Natal Reports

The Black Moon Lilith Natal Report

The Chiron Natal Report

Living in the Present Tense: A Personal Emotional
Healing Natal Report

ISBN 1453664645
EAN-13 9781453664643

CW01499855

CONTENTS

Introduction: Sacred Psychology

In the foreword to *The Soul's Journey I: Astrology, Reincarnation, and Karma with a Medium and Channel*, evolutionary astrologer Steven Forrest places my work in context of the emerging paradigms of sacred psychology. "[Insights] from disembodied beings combined with his own natural insights and his solid training in Evolutionary Astrology place [Tom] and this fine book on the cutting edge of not only Evolutionary Astrology, but also the emerging paradigms of sacred psychology.[1] These words have stuck with me and served as part of the inspiration to write this second volume of *Living Myth*.

Sacred psychology, as I understand it, is born from the marriage of the knowledge and data of the field of psychology with the wisdom gained from understanding ourselves as spiritual beings. As we grow into deeper awareness and expressions of our spiritual selves, the relevance of psychological modes of analysis will rest upon the ability of these modes

---

[1] Tom Jacobs, *The Soul's Journey I: Astrology, Reincarnation, and Karma with a Medium and Channel* (Tucson, AZ, 2011), 7.

not merely to *consider* the notion that we are spiritual beings but to *begin* with the fact that we are spiritual beings. To remain useful these modes of analysis will have to take as foundational the spiritual nature of human beings and seek to understand our psychological selves in terms of this truth.

While I here tell human stories and relate these stories to myths handed down throughout many generations, at its heart this book is really about sacred psychology. It explores the archetypal processes that we find ourselves living out in our daily lives that align with certain myths.[2] It seeks to see them through a lens that is both humanistic and spiritual. The material begins with the fact that we are spiritual beings having human experiences and then explores those human experiences as stories that we each unfold in the course of living. Each and every human being is on a spiritual path—whether we know it or not. The key to seeing this truth lies with our definition of the word "spiritual": if we believe that word is meant to point us to a deity outside ourselves, we likely will not see that energy and consciousness underlie everything. To understand ourselves as consciousness unfolding in a

---

[2] For a full treatment of the difference I see between myth (tools for social instruction) and archetype (how we live stories), see my book *Living Myth: Exploring Archetypal Journeys.*

search for understanding—how our souls see us—then we can upgrade our definition of "spiritual". We are on our way to understanding ourselves in terms of the energy that we are and *this*, in my eyes, is the first step toward a universal definition of "spiritual."

All of my work is centered on the fact that energy underlies and manifests everything in our lives. This is accepted in many healing disciplines that are contributing to defining what has become known as the *Quantum Age*. This age is the new paradigm we are edging into as we see and accept that energy is at the root and defining cause of everything. This way of seeing the world is evolving beyond Newtonian, mechanistic views of the world and our minds and bodies. For the last several hundred years we have, for example, become rooted in the idea that our bodies are machines with many interrelated processes and small parts that can break down for any number of reasons. This model was in place when psychoanalysis began with Freud in the 1890s and, in time, gained solid footing. Lists of complexes and discussion of all the things that can go wrong with humans psychologically can, in that paradigm, take precedence over the notion that we are beings with many interrelated facets. This fact can be covered over by the extensive intellectual analysis undertaken within the paradigm, accompanied by the human mind's endless pursuit of logic (presuming logic equals truth).

Indeed, the last few hundred years have left us wondering *if*—and often more or less believing *that*—we are bodies with minds (and/or spirits), and, as a result, we are spiritually sick. More than ever before, we are confused about what we are and who we are supposed to be, and it has everything to do with the cultural mindset that has led to how we do and speak the language of psychology.

We are on the cusp of a stage in our evolution in which we are coming to understand deeply and widely that we are energetic beings with physical manifestations. As we grasp this, we will see how health on all levels is influenced by energy. The Quantum Age as the next step in our collective evolution will reveal to us the interconnectedness of all parts of ourselves as well as all of life. What an exciting time to be a human!

On a personal note, each writing project I undertake is a learning experience. I have not yet come out on the other side of a natal report or book without having been changed by what I learned while writing it, even if I was intimately familiar with the material beforehand. *Living Myth: Exploring Archetypal Journeys* was, in part, a collection of monthly columns published on a website over a period of about a year. Some of the book's chapters were written one at a time and with a specific theme in mind. The remainder of the book was written to complete my original vision of the project, to include all the topics I didn't get to in the column's original run.

After completing that book and a few more, certain stories I've thought a lot about throughout my life have returned to mind. With the process of outlining the difference between myth and archetype now set in my mind, I began to think of these old(-to-me) stories in new ways.

Many of the stories included in *Living Myth: Exploring Archetypal Journeys* grew from my work in astrology (though that particular book is not much about astrology, save the final chapter on Arjunsuri). This present volume begins in a very different place—by beginning with the notion of exploring a spiritual psychology. It is important to me to help people understand the stories they are living, and that can happen without using astrology and/or other tools for self-understanding. The symbolic language used by those disciplines is very useful when it comes to working with myth and archetype in our lives and yet it is, of course, not the only route to understanding the human spiritual-psychological self.; so many incredible *a-has* can come from exploring deeply the stories that we *live*. This is the departure point for this present work.

As we explore archetypal stories and our relationships with them herein, you will find each tale related to a universal truth or spiritual principle. Our human tendencies and what we have been taught (usually implicitly) about each story will be contrasted with the archetypal thread about human nature and the universe to which it relates. This is the ground of sacred psychology: Viewing ourselves and our lives through the lens of our fundamental spiritual nature and how we simultaneously create and fit into the bigger plan. You will read about each story here in terms of a natural (spiritual) law that we can understand in order to shift our perspective on the story and why we live it.

These particular principles reflect what I have been learning along my own life (which is to say, *spiritual*) journey. Some or all might be familiar to you already. They are certainly not new, and I am not the first to teach something about them. You will find a handful of spiritual principles repeated, and you will see them come up in different contexts. We learn about each in our lives through a variety of experiences, and, in the various ways they find expression through humans, it can be useful to see them illustrated across the spectrum.

As I work toward orienting myself toward natural law and spiritual truth, I come back repeatedly to these principles, which allow me to dismantle the nonsense and misunderstanding I create in my day-to-day life and get on with living and working with what is true. These principles include, as an example, that all of our relationships serve to teach us about ourselves. It is easy to see those with whom we are involved as having an impact on us in one way or another, completely missing that they are really just showing us to ourselves. Letting that settle in and looking at your own relationships through that lens may result in a significant shift that would put you in more direct contact with an understanding of yourself as a spiritual being. You are powerfully creative, after all, and seeing each of your relationships as teaching you what your soul is asking that you learn changes how you think of and have relationships.

The Power of Choice

In addition to the ancient Hermetic maxim "As above, so below," we can also look to the universal law of "As within, so without." Such spiritual principles around which this book has been designed

11

enable us to know ourselves more and more deeply as the divine creative beings that we are. As Caroline Myss often points out in her work[3], each choice we make is an exercise of spiritual power, an act of creation. In order to know ourselves as Spirit or the Divine, we need to come to more conscious awareness of how our choices create the world around us.

In my experience, living in ways that are closely aligned with our spiritual selves requires us to understand our true motivations for doing anything that we do. We can be motivated by either faith or fear. As you read about myth and archetype in this book, you will encounter the repetition of the following questions: Are we making our choices based in fear or faith? And what follows from these choices? This is the single best way I have found to teach people how to live more closely aligned with their own spiritual natures. The more truth and conscious self-awareness you are "running," the less energy you are leaking through unhappy and damaging circumstances and choices in your life.

Spirituality also can be seen in terms of living in accordance with the aims and methods of one's soul.

---

[3] Caroline Myss, *Anatomy of the Spirit: The Seven Stages of Power and Healing* (New York, Penguin Random House LLC, 1996).

Souls operate only in alignment with love—they have no choice; it is their fundamental nature. Souls incarnate as humans and other animals to temporarily seem and feel disconnected from their true divine natures. They do this in order to learn, while embodied, how to return to the power of the loving state. Each of us, in other words, is here to learn to go from fear, pain, and sorrow into faith, acceptance, and compassion. We're here to learn to become the source of love for ourselves, and it is this process and its inherent aims that connects us to the wisdom of the soul and the divine consciousness operating in our lives.

As we live our lives somewhat aligned with the stories of mythological figures, we are making choices. In this book, as in *Living Myth: Exploring Archetypal Journeys*, I separate myth from archetype in order to show you what your choices are and offer you some ideas about new choices you might make when living one of these stories. You likely have been taught, directly and indirectly, that a mythic story always turns out in a particular way, and we are ready to cease being handicapped by this conditioning. What is true is that we embark on paths paralleling mythic figures but we get to choose how the stories turn out. The outcomes of myths are drilled into us during life and we can often repeat the ends of the stories by rote in a Pavlovian scenario that obviates the need for us to think for ourselves. *Myth is always social instruction, while archetype is the thread within the human psyche that must be lived out in order that we learn about how to be human and manage a wide variety of possible human experiences.* Any given social order depends on a stable of myths to teach its members how to be successful within the confines of its structure. And each member needs to learn the ropes and rules so as not to make the mistakes that would make them unwelcome in that social order.

My intention here begins with opening your eyes to seeing these stories in your life and in the lives of others. If you can understand the stories you are living—along with the subconscious expectations of their implied or necessary outcomes that you have absorbed from the collective unconscious as well as direct instruction—you can change how they unfold, and you can change your outcome. *You can decide what kind of life you want to live as you naturally draw from the collective consciousness the models for living that myths are.* Many of these handed-down myths are cautionary tales, telling us what not to do and how not to behave. At the same time, they provide natural models for us about how to live correctly. As a result, there is a lot of juice and use in finding out what they mean for us, collectively and individually.

Each of the stories here focuses on my reading of and feeling into how we live them. While I usually focus on one issue related to the archetypal journey, you might think of others, and I encourage you to allow this and to follow your hunches. Each and every myth can be stepped into in the ways you will find spelled out here, and each and every archetypal journey has multiple threads with which to work. Also, when we live a story, we tend to live a certain thread or two or three of that story and not always all of them. What I have chosen to focus on herein might not apply to your own life but I am sure you will be able to see the human story in it.

Another intention is to revive some interest in myth as a tool for self-understanding. The stories as we have received them do not always appeal to us or seem relevant to our post-modern lives, even as we seem to know deep down that they are or might be relevant. Looking at the archetypal process related to any myth, the story as we live it uncovers a lot of fodder for self-understanding. Working with our life stories in this way not only helps us choose directions and resolutions for certain arenas of our lives, it also supports us in feeling connected in ways that bypass our modern identities as attention-fractured, hyperaware consumers or gadget-users lost in the flow of data that constantly bombards us. Redeveloping a relationship with myths can lead us into more reflection and appreciation of what we as humans have in common, supporting us in inhabiting and grounding an idea of ourselves as part of the continuum of human social and cultural evolution.

Some of the questions myths encourage us to ask include *Who are we? Why are we here? What are we supposed to do with our lives? What makes a meaningful human life? How are we to make the right choices at the right times and for the right reasons?* It can become easy to avoid answering these questions and, even, to cease hearing them being asked within. They are so prevalent that they can become a source of white noise, with our awareness of them atrophying so that we don't have to feel inadequate because we cannot come up satisfying answers. Thereby, our identities as consumers can overshadow the part of the human self seeking meaning and understanding. Still, our increasing consumption has not eradicated this most natural of human needs.

The other intention I have for this book is to reveal ever more ways to decondition from who we have been told we are so that we can embrace who we *really* are. At present, I am focused on doing what

I can to dismantle the limitations of the patriarchy as they live within our psyches and energy fields. As a result, you will read much in this book about that system of social organization under which many on Earth have lived for thousands of years. While this book can seem to be about busting open some myths, it is also about busting open the philosophy and teaching tools of the patriarchy, with the end goal that we return to accepting ourselves for being precisely who we are and loving that—reclaiming the right of self-definition. We are ready to be empowered and take our selves, lives, and hearts back from the culture shapers of six thousand years ago as they embarked on a human experiment that has clearly proven itself not worth continuing. It has been the job of those feeding and upholding the current system of social management we call patriarchy to teach us who to be and who not to be, yet we are currently evolving beyond the need to be told who we are.

As a philosophy undergraduate, I was a fan of the variety of existentialism that stated, "Okay, so there's no meaning in the world around you. What are you going to *do* about it? What are you going to create in order to have meaning?" This is reflected in the ideas of Albert Camus, which you will read about in the chapter, *Penelope and Sisyphus: Why Bother?* With a heavy Sagittarian and 9th-house signature in my natal chart, I find myself "deeply concerned" with "questions of meaning." Coming to see that we have free will in every moment healed the twists and roller coasters of mind that had me confused about why I am here, what I am to be doing, and how I am supposed to live. So, for me, it's not worth investing in or doing anything if there's no way to create a meaningful path. This way of teasing apart myth and archetype offers endless opportunities to create such paths, and so I'm happy to be able to share these thought processes and what I've come up with about living these stories and choosing better outcomes than our myths may imply are our destinies.

This approach to myth and the notion of sacred psychology takes me back to the kind of excitement I had when I was confronted with the challenge of creating meaning if I wanted to have it. In the context of the stories explored here, if you live an Orpheus story, do you create the meaning that you lose what you love or do you create the meaning that you need to learn to trust the bigger picture? If you live a Pallas Athene story, are you creating meaning through loyalty as you try to be something that seems noble but that isn't realistic and authentic? We are all creating meaning as we live these stories. We are all *already* doing it. I intend this book to illuminate some ways to turn the narrative you are creating into something that is positively meaningful to you and that supports you in living a more peaceful, self-aware, and intentional life.

In the following chapters, we will explore the following myths:

- *Adam and Eve: Our Favorite Dom and Sub.* Culturally acceptable versions of man and woman.

- *Orpheus: Fear vs. Faith.* Roles of trust, grief, loss, and faith in the Divine Plan.

- *Pallas Athene: Daddy's Little Girl.* Loyalty to the father as disavowal of the female lineage.

- *Eris: Pushing Buttons and Lighting Fires.* Provoking insecurities and causing discord as a way to heal social rejection issues.

- *Paris and the Power of Choice.* Reality-show dating games, prizes, and the real meaning of power.

- *Iphigenia's Sacrifice.* Parent-child dynamics, "losing" a child, tribal attitudes.

- *Don Juan and Dionysus:* Lovers of Women. Beyond seduction and drunkenness, these gods serve the Goddess.

- *Prometheus: "Knowledge is Power" and the Gift of Innovation.* Genius, power, fire-stealing, and liver-eating.

- *Nessus: Living in Two Worlds.* "Carrying" others, animal urges, misrepresentation, oh my.

- *Penelope and Sisyphus: Why Bother?* Repetition, eternity, absurdity, doing, and undoing as they relate to the creative act.

- Oedipus: Pain, Karma, and the Fallacy of Destiny. Family stories, bloodlines, "fate," and why seeds of energy hold more power than DNA in determining the future.

One final note: Four of the first five sections of this volume (Introduction, Adam and Eve, Orpheus, and Eris) were edited by Jillian Sheridan. My thanks go to her keen eye and superpowers when it comes to finding the right words and nudging me toward evolving into a better writer. All errors, gaffes, and issues that remain are mine.

Adam and Eve: Our Favorite Dom and Sub

My thoughts on Adam and Eve evolved from my exploration of the truth behind the Lucifer and Lilith stories we inherited. I often work with these four as a quartet representing culturally acceptable versions of masculine and feminine (Adam and Eve) versus culturally unacceptable versions (Lucifer and Lilith).[4] Therefore, this chapter will focus on Adam and Eve but include much discussion of the contrasts with Lucifer and Lilith.

Adam and Eve are offered as the acceptable models for men and women, respectively. They are who we are supposed to think we are if we are going to do well in social contexts defined by Judeo-Christian mores and teachings. By emphasizing, through Adam and Eve, the virtues of going with the flow and following cultural instructions, Lucifer and

---

[2] For a full treatment of the difference I see between myth (tools for social instruction) and archetype (threads of consciousness within the psyche), see *Living Myth: Exploring Archetypal Journeys*. For more on Lilith and Lucifer, see the Black Moon Lilith Natal Report, the book *Lilith: Healing the Wild*, and the Living in the Present Tense Natal Report.

Lilith become shadow archetypes. Shadows are parts of ourselves we are afraid to look at in case they turn out to be real. If we did, everything would have to change, we'd be dangerous sorts of people, we'd be rejected and alone, we'd be unloved, etc. In other words, we would, in some way, find survival difficult or impossible. Creating shadows out of (naturally occurring) parts of ourselves, however, always leads to distortion and manifests as imbalance and a lack of self-knowledge, self-acceptance, and self-love. In a sense, our shadows become our devils, and the knots, fears, and tensions they carry are what bring us to do unhealthy things, i.e., "bad things."

The short story is that Lilith and Lucifer are difficult, if not impossible, to control. When healthy, they slough off the cultural instructions of how to define the self and how to behave, doing what they need to do for their own reasons. Sometimes this overlaps with cultural instruction but sometimes it doesn't. Because Lilith and Lucifer represent threats to cultures grown out of and based in Judeo-Christian ideals and mores, those cultures demonize these archetypes and do what they can to keep regular folk from identifying with them in healthy ways. These folk, then, end up not accepting what they know is true about themselves (how they are naturally wired) as good and right and proper. This is deeply damaging to many people over time (and over many lifetimes—because we all carry the memories of our soul's other human lives).

The cultural distortions surrounding the feminine (including sexual violence and the sex trade) are sourced in this misunderstanding. It is time that we finally get to the bottom of these myths as vehicles for social instruction so that we can become empowered to define ourselves openly according to who we really are and leave behind all damaging ideas, laws, expectations, mores, and fears.

We are not taught that Adam and Eve are mythological figures because we take (or come from people or contexts that take) the Judeo-Christian mythos and scriptures seriously. We mostly consider the stories from which they came as holy texts, and we may do so even if we do not subscribe to the associated religions. In my estimation, this is partly out of respect for these cultural tropes that surround us that we have not opened to consider Adam and Eve as mythological figures. I believe the thinking is akin to this: *Such figures seem to us to belong to the old days, when we had many stories about many gods. We no longer need whatever they were about because now we are living according to the (patriarchal, Newtonian, postmodern, or whatever) truth.* Despite this, they remain as models of behavior to teach us certain dos and don'ts.

The Ideals

The ideal expression of the archetype of Adam is to be upstanding, upright, respectable, concerned for the community, respectful of his betters, and responsible for his commitments. A person lives as a healthy Adam when he or she is responsible, follows through on commitments, and treats his or her family in loving but firm, structured, and directing ways. Adam people do what is expected of them by the higher-ups and give instruction to those Eves and young Adams around them who are not yet or at all capable or not qualified to make decisions and take care of important things on their own. The ideal Adam holds the world together through his activity, intentions, commitments, and responsibilities.

The ideal expression of the Eve archetype is to be flexible, attentive, and supportive of what the Adam in his or her life wants, needs, and is about. An Eve is committed to furthering what an Adam is committed to furthering and believes what that Adam believes (or goes along with it if not). A good Eve takes instruction humbly and does not assert his or her own opinions if these opinions clash with those of Adam. A person lives an Eve story when he or she sacrifices his or her own goals and personal voice in support of someone else's agenda, does what that person wants and needs, or is willing to fold or *does* fold his or her goals and voice into that of Adam. The ideal Eve holds the world together through her deference, humility, commitment, and silence.

We are all exposed to these ideals as we grow up. Many of us are directly shaped to be good Adams and Eves by our families, schools, communities, and other routes to conditioning. Not all of us are surrounded by instruction and pressure to turn out this way and, among those of us who are, the teaching doesn't always stick. Each human has an individual soul and karmic journey that determines everything about how these pressures are encountered and responded to.

It is important to note that the changes in family and social definitions and structures over the last several decades has lessened the power that this conditioning imperative has over us. I speak about it as if it is more widely prevalent than many might see to be true. I do so in this way because as energetic beings, we carry energies with us that are associated with our souls' many lives. These energies are experienced as emotions. In important ways each of us is the product or manifestation of the emotions we have, which are the energies carried in our energetic fields. We are all trying to come out of the destruction of the patriarchy in one way or another, and these attitudes are extremely prevalent in us as a collective, even as society and family dynamics are changing over time to support more individuality and less control-oriented mechanisms for conditioning.

As we live these journeys as individuals, if we encounter this instruction as pressure, then it is important for us at the soul level to do so. Each soul has for the last six thousand years known that its human manifestations will be dealing with these issues, including fairness, equality, respect, autonomy, right and healthy sexuality, and other virtues encompassed by the Adam and Eve dynamic. This struggle to figure out how to be the right kind of woman or man is an extension of a universal issue that souls come to Earth to explore, which is how to live as a human.

The bottom line is that we are all exposed to these models as ideals of who we can turn out to be, and we all have free will about how we should respond. Many of our souls' journeys hinge on these issues, in fact. The souls incarnating on Earth now can see the social fabric and moral philosophies that are in play in all the various Earth cultures over time. Whatever a person is experiencing when it comes to figuring out whether and how to be Adam and Eve (and Lilith and Lucifer) fits with the soul's plan.

When They Go Wrong

Adam goes wrong when he does not listen to his higher-ups, when he for some reason does not take responsibility for his actions or is not upstanding. He also goes wrong when he does not guide or lead others around him who are not capable or qualified to guide and lead themselves and others, when he or she fails in not providing leadership and giving moral instruction to his or her Eves and little Adams.

Eve goes wrong when she or he for some reason does not comply with what Adam tells him or her to do, and when he or she asserts thoughts, ideas, beliefs, and opinions that challenge or counter what Adam believes. Eve goes wrong when she believes that she or he exists for reasons that have to do primarily with her- or himself, when she or he asserts the self and claims the right to have a destiny or create a path that differs from the one Adam might have already chosen for him or her.

When we see these two go wrong, we are taught various ways of helping them get back on track. After all, it seems in all of our best interests to make as many Adams and Eves as possible, as the social structures in Western culture are built around these prescriptions for conception of self. We are taught from a young age that success is a direct result of boys being good Adams and girls being good Eves. In some ways it doesn't matter if a person was raised in a progressive family environment, attended progressive schools, and/or hooked up with progressive people. The cultural instruction makes it into every environment in one way or another, and it is the prevailing one in which we are raised that shapes us, no matter our or our family's politics, beliefs, and objections to its teachings.

Our Favorite Dom and Sub

My use of this phrase with these two figures is only a little tongue-in-cheek. We have been shaped culturally to know that things go well for us and everyone around us when we live up to the expectations of being good Adams and Eves, depending on our gender. Yet when we do, it is most definitely a dom/sub relationship. Adam is the dom. His job is to tell Eve what to do. Eve's job is to listen. Eve's job is to submit.

Yet the deeper level of these dynamics that we need to see is that Adam is also a sub. While his job is to tell Eve what to do, *he* gets instructions from above, too. He is told by the culture creators and shapers what he needs to tell Eve to do. The patriarchal god as he lives in the minds and hearts of the people shaped over time by these social conventions is always ready to give Adam instructions on how to live and behave and what he should be doing with his Eves and little Adams. And Eve takes her instructions from Adam, never seeking to go outside the accepted chain of command.

Adam can be successful in this culture if he or she does what the more powerful and qualified Adams in his or her life tell him or her to do. Eve is caught at the bottom of the food chain, and Adam is caught in the middle. A very few number of Adams can in fact rise to the status of culture creator and shaper and so succeeding in this paradigm affords some freedom to not many at any given time. But for everyone else involved, it is a series of traps that have to do with making sure that everyone knows who the biggest Adams are in the immediate environment and that everyone knows exactly what those Adams want of everyone else.

When everyone does what they are supposed to do according to this scheme, life functions as a well-oiled machine. Everyone gets precisely where he or she needs to be at the right times, provided that it has been thought up, controlled, and/or sanctioned by an Adam somewhere along the line. Everyone gets precisely what he or she wants and needs, as long as these are defined, shaped, corrected, and/or approved of by an Adam. And yet even when this is all going smoothly, there is a feeling of something missing. There is a feeling that something somehow isn't quite right.

While some Adams and Eves accept that what they are told about themselves is true, others long for something new and fresh to come in and offer an alternative view of who they are. There are really just two kinds of Adams and two kinds of Eves: 1) Those who accept what they are being fed about who they are and live lives that are only partially fulfilling, and 2) those who seek to grow beyond the patriarchal contexts and discover and live out the truth behind who they really are.

Reaching out for answers means going against what culture shapers for thousands of years have attempted to instill in us as fear of finding out something other than what we have been taught. For those who live in stricter moral climates—including those adhering to the teachings of traditional religions—this can be a dangerous prospect. They can risk being rejected by their people or support structures by seeking out new answers to old questions. For many of us, however, we might be a generation or two (or more) removed from strict adherence to religious laws and mores.

For those who wish to evolve beyond old explanations but do not because of social or family pressure, the impulse to grow becomes stifled. The need to find out that it is in fact right and appropriate to love the self for being just who one is, how one is wired, remains unmet. And this leads in every case to distortion.

True Natures

Distorted Adams and Eves lead to a sort of chaos, and this automatically brings us to Lucifer and Lilith – the other sides of the coins. As I stated earlier, I think about these four as a quartet because when those of us living the socially sanctioned versions of masculine and feminine (Adam and Eve) look inside, we can't help but find the other two staring back at us. Conversely, when Lucifer and Lilith look inside they find Adam and Eve staring back, and this can be just as confusing. Yet because of the nature of the culturally derived and maintained split within our hearts and minds about these ways of being, we might not always be clear how to be and accept all four energies within us.

We are in fact complete beings, and that we see the others when we look inside with absolutely open eyes is the core of the nature of being human. That Lucifer and Lilith are shadows is due only to our willingness to keep them out of our emotional, psychological, and sexual mainstreams; to keep these vital and vibrantly alive parts of us shamed and hidden. When we give ourselves permission to be whole, each of us can reclaim the self as an amalgam of these four archetypes, leaving behind forever the fear, control games, and moral sanctioning we have instituted, thrown at each other, and absorbed over the last six millennia.

If we are to take back the power to be open to experiencing who we truly are, we need to make peace with the history of this ungrounded and unhealthy dom/sub culture that has been passed off as the only acceptable sort of reality. These teachings that a woman can succeed if she listens to a man and that a man can succeed if he keeps her in line according to the instruction he has received from bigger men are not possibly supportive of who we are as energetic beings, as conscious selves ever seeking growth and change. If we want to change the world and end the destructive agenda that is the patriarchy, we have to be willing to see all of ourselves … accept what we see … *and honor what we see*. We need to celebrate who we really are and commit to bringing it out in self and other.

This means taking the rebellious, bad-boy energy of Lucifer and giving it some direction by opening to love. It means taking the wild-woman energy of Lilith and releasing it within and between us in the spirit of love. It means being willing to be responsible for others when it is appropriate to be Adam, yet leave others to learn about and define themselves and make choices on their own because they are respected as beings unto themselves—not tools for the production of good little myopic, closed-hearted, confused, and sad Adams and Eves. Finally, it means being willing to be the best of the respectful and interested-in-others side of Eve while remaining always committed to speaking our truth (no matter what), respecting who we truly are, and never choosing to be stepped on for any reason.

And this is possible, even if everything you have been taught your entire life (over many lifetimes) is a broken record stuck on the contrary. You can take back your life from the confused musings of the culture shapers from six thousand years ago. You can give yourself permission to be whole.

When you do this, you will change the world.

Orpheus: Fear vs. Faith

Orpheus is heralded as a master lyre player who can charm anyone with his playing. People, animals, rocks, and trees alike are pacified and softened by the beauty of his music. The story of Orpheus we know best surrounds the death and near-resurrection of his one true love Eurydice, and that is the one we will explore here.

In the myth, Eurydice is out and about with her friends when she is spied by Aristaeus as a most desirable female. In her flight from his unwelcome advances, she is bitten by a poisonous snake and dies. At this point, Eurydice and Orpheus have been married only a short time.

With Eurydice's death seemingly before her time, Orpheus descends into a deep grief. He decides that he simply cannot let her go—he cannot live without her. He fixes to go to the Underworld to play a mournful song there for the Lord and Lady (Hades and Proserpine) as a request to let Eurydice be allowed to come back to the world of the living and rejoin him to live a long life as they had intended. He believes that the depth and purity of his love as contained in his song will be deemed worthy of this gift. He could not be more convinced of the power of the love he has for his dead bride.

Orpheus makes this journey, and his song touches the hearts of the King and Queen of the dead, which is no mean feat. His wish is granted with one condition: As Orpheus and Eurydice travel back to the world of the living together, Orpheus must go first, and he must not look back at Eurydice. He must not turn around to see if she is still there—not even once. If he does, she will be drawn forever back to the Underworld and remain dead. And, if that happens, there will be no possible recourse no matter what Orpheus or anyone else does.

And, so, turning around to see if Eurydice is still there is, of course, precisely what Orpheus does do on the journey to the surface. Eurydice is at that moment sucked back down to the depths and Orpheus loses her forever. He could not help but look back to make sure she was there, so intent was he on being reassured that he had actually been granted this gift from the gods of the dead.

After this second loss of her, he never recovers.

Orpheus's tale comes to us then as one of woe. It is a story of true love and true loss, of death, and of going to great lengths to try to undo what cannot (and perhaps should not) be undone.

As we live Orpheus's story, we focus on and are learning through living a handful of main threads.

Trust

The story of Orpheus is about trust but in more than one sense. That Orpheus does not trust that Eurydice is behind him is why he turns to look. This evidences a lack of trust, yes, but there is more: Orpheus cannot, when Eurydice dies, trust that it is in fact her time to die. He allows his grief to overtake him and he sets about to undo what has never before been undone: Going to the Underworld to ask its Lord to let someone come back to life. In some sense, this is the very definition of crazy. It is an act of desperation that reveals a fundamental lack of trust in life and the universe.

The Power of Love

Orpheus might seem to trust in the power of love but this would be a contemporary interpretation of the story by those influenced by all manner of media from any of the Brontës all the way up to John Hughes, Nicholas Sparks, and pop and country music of all flavors: *Love conquers all. Love will triumph. If you truly love, you are willing to do anything, move mountains, and wait for your beloved no matter what happens or how long it takes. If you really love someone you'll go to hell to get her back.* The message is that if you are not willing to go to extraordinary lengths that scare the hell out of normal people—including going to literal hell—then you're not doing it right. You might not, in fact, really *love* that person.

Orpheus's story is lived by the broken-hearted who cannot imagine themselves without their beloved other. All those who define themselves in terms of their relationships run the risk of living Orpheus stories that can blossom into monumental grief. We love love, we need love, we crave love— but our definition of love needs attention here. If we define ourselves in terms of the apparent safety we derive from the presence of a loved one, then we're not loving so much as clinging to something that keeps us from being alone and/or attempting to put our ability to feel whole and complete onto another person. Despite Orpheus's depth of love, he carries a deep fear of being alone or incomplete and from this we can take important notes.

"Romance" is a cultural inheritance we're all in need of growing beyond. The mythos of romantic love holds that you're saved if someone comes along and loves you, and you're safe on an ongoing basis if that person stays with you. You are validated as a human (attractive, kind, interesting, intelligent, loving, etc.) by being chosen, and it is assumed this will continue as long as that other person continues to choose you. This construct is based in a perception that each person is separate from the divine, from the God consciousness that we each contain and that he or she is somehow incomplete. Its myths have to do with ensuring that we know either that there's something fundamentally wrong with us (from the Christian mythos) or that we can't possibly be strong enough to live life on our own.

As it happens from the perspective of souls, other people come into our lives when we need something activated within us, and they leave when either it's been activated or we know what it is and can step forward to own and embrace it. Each person has numerous agreements between his or her soul and those of others to help drive his or her evolution. No soul can come to Earth and live as a human without the help of many other souls doing the same thing! There's so much to learn about ourselves as souls living human lives, and others are necessary along all of our individual learning journeys. Where we go wrong is when we invest in others (or The Other) so much power to validate us that we don't know how to go on without them.

Whatever Eurydice opened up in Orpheus, he couldn't see how to own the wholeness of himself that she showed him and he therefore couldn't let her go. This is a common thread in the human evolution story as we learn about how to own what others light up and bring out of us, taking back the power of love by owning what our soul knows: Each of us is living on Earth to remember how to become the source of love for the self. Love is the true nature of soul, and we're here to remember this while in human form and processing human thoughts, beliefs, and emotions.

The shadow of romantic love gets airtime only after a new romantic relationship's shine begins to fade. There's no definitive timeline for this fading, but it happens. Some will see this time as a chance to mature beyond naïve, adolescent expectations of relationships (ahem, "romance") and others as a failure of themselves, the other, or the entire system of love, or the unnecessary cruelty of the universe itself. Orpheus's story sits firmly in the romantic love mythos that we've been handed down for so long in order to have some way of knowing how to measure the power of the love we ourselves carry: If you're not willing to go to hell and back for her, you probably don't really love her.

Why would we need such a measure? I believe it has to do with an innate need each human has in order to feel that life has meaning and purpose. We each need to know that we're here for a reason but have been taught that the source of meaningfulness is always outside us. If we feel thoroughly broken by the loss of a great love—perhaps our One and Only True Love—then at least it can appear that our life was worth living. We can then have a sense that we did something of value, that we had the wisdom and courage to invest in something worth investing in.

Owning the power of self-love is the key to coming out of these stuck places in which the Orpheus myth can tell us we're supposed to dwell, and doing so fulfills the mission each of us is here to perform: To become the source of love for ourselves while human.

Fear vs. Faith

Orpheus lacks faith. He chooses not to imagine that there is a greater order into which Eurydice's death fits. He does not trust because he does not want to give up the happiness and identity that he derives from being with Eurydice. The news flash for Orpheus (and those of us who live his story) is that everything changes: *People die. Everyone dies. Everyone you know will die. Yes, even you will die.*

Are you so wrapped up in who you get to be with that you cannot imagine letting them go when their time has come?

In the story, fear is the motivation for all Orpheus does. His project is therefore lost before he even goes to Hades armed with his lyre and his aching, moaning, grieving heart.

When we live this story, the mission is lost when we give more power to the fear of change than the faith in the perfection of the unfolding plan of life—faith in the universe, of our souls and those with whom we create emotionally entangled, beautiful, and tragic stories of both life and death.

How much power do you give the presence in your life of your loved ones?

How much power do you lose when someone you care for leaves your life, through leaving, abandonment, or death?

How much of your power and life force are you willing to lose through grief? From refusing to move on?

Endeavors based in fear never lead to love. The intention with which we step into a situation always dictates its outcome. If Orpheus were to go to Hades with the faith that what is best for all is what will unfold, then he would have no need to turn around to see if his beloved was still there. If he were to make this journey from a place of love, he would experience a reunion with a wonderful part of himself, the part that he believes has died with his beloved Eurydice. But he doesn't. He can't. His self-definition as grief-stricken and lost has taken over, and he dives into his unprecedented journey running on the fuel of fear.

Hades grants Orpheus's wish with the single condition that he not turn around once before reaching the surface. I think Hades does this because Orpheus has come not out of love but from fear. He has come to ask for his bride to be brought back to life so that he himself can be relieved of suffering. This is an important point for us, because when we, as does Orpheus, confuse the depth of pain of loss for love, we handicap ourselves and set ourselves up for further pain. This can teach us the important lesson of discerning between fear and faith and learning that our personal power rests in choosing to transition over time through many individual choices from fear into faith. For the Orpheus within us, it's a difficult choice to surrender such a closely-guarded identity.

Can we keep faith? Can we choose to have faith that everything will turn out the way that it needs to? Can we step away from fear of pain that creates the desperate scenarios such that which Orpheus finds himself hastily rushing into? Can we live from and into faith that all that happens serves the highest good of all, even when we experience the worst sorts of loss and pain?

All Things Die, But All Things Need to Die

It is the way of the world, the way of life. We energetic beings having physical experiences living as humans are said never to die. Some of our religious traditions teach us of the immutability of the spirit, the transmigration of souls that is a great wheel upon which we all turn many, many times. Yet in the context of us as humans, everything does die. It is the only guarantee we have once we are born. Can we trust this? Are we willing to participate in life while we are here and then let it go? Are we willing to participate in the lives of others as long as they are with us and then let them go?

The Divine Plan

Orpheus's story calls up in us the question of whether there is a divine plan or at least a plan bigger than the one we have set out for ourselves. It asks us to look at where we have placed our faith and if, in fact, we have any. Since it is a story of loss, we are also tasked when living this archetypal thread to learn the very human lesson of why we think special others come into our lives and why they leave. We have to look at our beliefs about the timing of these entrances and exits.

Again, the truth from the perspective of soul is that people enter our lives when we need a particular sort of teaching, when we need a particular kind of life teacher to affect us. The other half of it is that they leave when we no longer need them, when we have either learned the lesson or, at least, been exposed to the opportunity to learn it and refused, putting it off to another time. There are important others in our lives who make an entrance to give us the chance to learn something through relating with them, yet we always and in each moment have free will. If we refuse a lesson, it is common for the teacher who has entered our lives solely to teach it to find somewhere else to go, whether in this world or the next. Living Orpheus's story leaves us needing to answer the question about why these people have come in and why they leave when they do and how they do.

Our orientation to the notion of a divine plan after having been affected for so many millennia by patriarchal religion leaves us a little confused about this truth. There is a divine plan many are willing to acknowledge, but it is in fact one of our own devising: a mythos meant to keep us loyal to whatever religiopolitical force happens to be in charge at the time. We as souls are the prime movers in our lives; there is no power greater than and outside us that is in fact calling the shots, pulling the strings of our lives. Yet we are in a long-term process of learning this, of empowering ourselves to make our own choices and learn through dealing with the consequences.

Identities Within and Through Relationship

We can choose to define ourselves by what we have and love (including the presence of loved ones) and by what and who we lose. It can be easy to create identities based in our relationships, but let's take a lesson from Orpheus: *We are each, in truth, complete unto ourselves. Those we love—those who have a significant, life-changing impact upon us—are teachers who come on the scene to teach us something we need to learn. When the lesson is complete, we all transition into the future, one way or another.*

When we insist on identifying as what is lost or the feeling of loss, as giving into being defined by loss, what we have actually lost is the ability to identify as the kind of person who has the right to exist in wholeness as who we really are. In this state, it seems as we've lost the willingness to continue, as to do so would mean going into and fully embracing the pain we feel, a fate seemingly worse than death. We feel an emptiness because who we got to be in that relationship seems no longer possible because the person who brought it out of us, the apparent creator of our happy or perfect state of being, is now gone. When in this position, we need to wake up to the fact of what has actually happened. We need to grieve the loss but also to recognize the dynamic we shared with that other person as an important learning experience.

From here, I invite you to look at why you are in the relationships you are in. Why have you chosen them? What do you hope to get from them? Then, what do you expect them to provide you?

It is normal and natural to find that we are having the relationships we are so that we get to be more whole, so that we get to be all of ourselves. It is also normal and natural that others bring out the best in us. The trick is in taking responsibility for these more whole versions of ourselves once we see others reflecting ourselves to us. When we fail to do this, we set ourselves up for the intensity of loss and grief that Orpheus embodies.

Once you take responsibility for yourself, for all these various versions of you that others have reflected to you over the course of your life, relationships can now be seen as vehicles for celebration. We get into them because of love, then we let our projections take over and we can forget to celebrate. When we relieve others of the responsibility of making us whole—of enabling us to finally get on with being more of who we really are—then we are free to enjoy our relationships for what we have always intended them to be: Sharing, expressing, and celebrating love as we learn about life and each other together.

If you are in this sort of self-responsible and loving space with others, you position yourself to be able to accept that everything changes. You no longer fear losing yourself if you happen to lose relationships that are important to you. You are open to being grateful for the impact that others have on you, and you appreciate the opportunity to have impacts on them.

In this space, you are able to experience all of your important relationships as the gifts that they are. In these relationships, you can offer and receive the gift of reflection and resultant self-revelation. It is true that we need each other to see who we ourselves truly are.

We as Orpheus need to open to being willing to be changed by experience. Orpheus shares this in common with Persephone,[5] a figure who cannot avoid being changed by time and experience. When we live an Orpheus story, we owe it to ourselves to look at loss as one more chapter of learning, one more opportunity to experience who we are and who we have become as a result of our most important relationships. In whatever ways we are invested in the present moment becoming a static future, we will without exception be shocked into something new, one way or another. Everything changes. Everything dies. Each and every one of us has to move on.

These relationships are gifts. Can we appreciate them for what they are *while* they are part of our lives?

When Not to Let Go

All that said, we also have to learn when *not* to let go. We can learn from both sides of this as we live Orpheus stories. There are times when it is absolutely healthy to fight for something that is important to us.

If we let something go because we recognize it is time for it or our attachment to it to die, great! This is mature and healthy. This leads us into growth in

---

[5] See Volume I for the chapter "Persephone's Ransom."

whatever directions we need: We opened to what we experienced and, when it was done, we let it go. We are then living in harmony with the divine plan as set out by our souls. In this way, we live in rhythm with how our lives need to unfold, and higher-level learning follows from people coming into our lives for good reason and leaving when their mission regarding us is complete.

Yet if we let something go because we feel overpowered by circumstance or another, perhaps we need to learn to stand up and fight for what is truly important to us. Some of us are learning life journeys about asserting ourselves and about making our desires and needs important.

When it comes to living Orpheus stories, we have to be clear about our motivations. If we are driven by fear, we must take the opportunity to evolve. We simply have to let go of the idea that particular others are necessary for us to feel whole. If you go to Hades with fear in your heart, Hades will overpower you. If, on the other hand, you are driven by love and faith, then there is something to be done. There are points in everyone's life when it is in fact mature and healthy to make a stand and fight for what is important. Approaching Hades with love in your heart, you are open to receiving the answer from the gods that best suits your learning journey as a divine being figuring out the right ways to live a human life.

Pallas Athene: Daddy's Little Girl

The first volume in this series contains a chapter titled "Pallas Athene and Reintegration". In it I take a look at the goddess's disavowal of her maternal lineage when she attests in open court that she was born from her father and there was no woman involved, which is called *parthenogenesis*. Her femininity is, therefore, in a way put on a shelf. She attempts to divorce herself from that part of her life, but her femininity can never, in truth, go away. As we live that side of her story, there is a part of us we attempt to divorce ourselves from in order to be more successful in a certain context. In this chapter you'll read about another side of Pallas Athene's story: loyalty to her father. It's part of the disavowal of her female lineage in open court, but it seems to call for more attention on its own in the specific thread related to daddy's little girl, which can also manifest as mommy's little boy. Feel free to substitute the latter as you read if that resonates with you.

Daddy's Little Girl: The Basics

This thread of Pallas Athene's story is present when she aligns with her father at the trial, which includes a denial of her matrilineal heritage. Pallas Athene states under pressure from her father and others in court that she was born from her father's head fully formed and armored, and that no woman was involved.

Most of what comes to me when I consider what the daddy's little girl thread means makes me uneasy, telling me there is a lot to unravel. This story begins with the idea that a daughter is to be protected and the father is the one to do it. It makes sense for a portion of a daughter's life, but eventually she needs to grow beyond the limitations of her father's influence, and the relationship needs to change. We don't talk about this pattern when it comes to seven year-old girls because it is appropriate at that age. Kids, after all, do need protection. When it continues into the teenage years, we get why it's still there and tend not to judge it, but if it continues into adulthood we can see that it becomes less appropriate.

There is a teaching in some corners of our collective mind that women cannot take care of themselves. This comes from thousands of years lived through the lens of patriarchy, a social philosophy based in elevating the masculine in order to get certain things accomplished, necessarily diminishing the feminine along the way.[6] Equally entrenched can be the assumption that girls never really grow up or become competent and able to make their own decisions, relieving us of the need to think of any female human as a woman. Living from within this old thread of patriarchal thinking, it's easier that males make decisions for females in order to ensure that the right decisions for them are made. During the history of living within this paradigm, we have mostly denied female humans the option of making their own decisions and, so, feel we are naturally justified in assuming they're not competent enough to make the right ones. While we consider ourselves thoroughly modern people, this patriarchal imbalance is in our roots.

The energetic container in the collective that we can call "daddy's little girl" is a solution to these assumed problems: Fathers are to take care of and protect their daughters until, presumably, another man comes forward to do it. This would normally be a husband, of course, but could also be another family member. Where daddy's little girl is pronounced in a family dynamic, the bar for the right kind of man to

---

[6] See *Goddess Past, Present, and Future* for a channeled explanation for the genesis of the patriarchy and *Lilith: Healing the Wild* for an astrological teaching of the same.

take over care and feeding of the daughter can be extremely high. The new man has to be just as good as daddy.

From the standpoint of the father, the new man has to be good enough to match the father's motivations, methods, and abilities. But that new man can't be *better* than the father, as that would reveal that the father isn't perfect, which is to say the right kind of man. (This is all based on the two parties worshipping each other as perfect, as idealized super beings neither could ever turn out to be.) The father, therefore, has to scrutinize the qualities and quality of the daughter's potential husbands while remaining on the lookout for any of them who might challenge the mythology of the father's own high, exemplary quality. Because, it must be said at this point, no father is perfect, but built into the daddy's little girl fantasy is that every father *is* by virtue of being the father who is looking out for the daughter. Inevitably, it becomes obvious to anyone willing to see even a tiny bit of reality that no father is perfect, but the emotional structure between daddy and his little girl must be maintained so that each can carry the illusion that what he wants for her is only the best.

The father also has to do what he can to train the new man to keep the daughter in line, to keep her the precious and perfect treasure he himself has spent so many years cultivating. The father must impart to the new man what exactly it is that counts as appropriate treatment of her, but also how to benefit from the years of conditioning the father has brought to shape the daughter so that she can meet his expectations (as well as those of any man the father would deem as appropriate for her to be handed off to). She has, after all, allowed herself to be molded into what her father expects her to be, and this will not be wasted upon any man the father will not deem to be the right sort of new man to take over her care and feeding.

From the standpoint of the daughter, daddy always has her best interests in mind. *She* knows she's not perfect, but if she can keep living within the parameters of his expectation and estimation of what makes a girl a good girl, everything will be fine. Keeping daddy happy is the ideal outcome so she can ensure that she's taken care of—at minimum so that she can survive—but there's often more involved about lifestyle and permissions to be out and participate in the world in certain ways. If she fulfills the terms of this contract, daddy will make sure that she is not just taken care of in the short term, but that he hands her off to the right kind of new man somewhere down the road, a man who will continue the care and feeding she's become accustomed to with daddy.

Virtue, the Hymen, and Sexuality

Just as every daddy knows he's not as perfect as the deal calls on him to be, every girl knows that she's not as perfect as the deal calls on her to be. There's a difference between their positions here, though, because the father has years of experience that the daughter does not. He likely is better at maintaining the façade that he's holding up his part of the bargain, but also he has the power: He is the one who defines the deal in terms of his expectations of the daughter, while the daughter grows into a young woman with emotions, hormones, curiosities, and opinions that may clearly not fit within the deal that the father set up years ago, at or even before her birth. So, the daughter is always disadvantaged in the daddy-little girl deal, as she is automatically expected to live up to an ideal that she doesn't really know if she can live up to.

For instance, can any teenager avoid the biochemical-emotional swells and swoons that can be stirred by attractive and intriguing others? Part of being the right kind of daughter in patriarchal society is not engaging in sexual activity with anyone the family hasn't chosen for her. Even if she doesn't get busy with anyone, being attracted to or piqued by a peer—or, heaven forbid!, someone ten or twenty years older!—can show signs that may be interpreted by daddy as threatening to veer off the path of propriety. We know that this is because daddy knows exactly how it feels to be tempted to stray off the path by some hot little thing, both when he was that young and now.

And that brings us to the treasure that the father has been cultivating the daughter to be the whole time, the crux of what it means to be a good girl: virginity. At some point, each child growing into adulthood has to decide if he or she is going to be remain loyal to long-held expectations of his or her family over recognizing the reality of how he or she is changing as an individual in the given time. Each young person must confront his or her unique wiring and individual nature. This comes out nearly universally through the advent of sexual behavior, but also is played out when a child in a religious or political family environment realizes that he or she cannot toe the family's party line, simply follow in its groove. And it plays itself out in the minds and hearts of all young people who realize that they are wired to experience sexuality in some way other than heterosexuality (or gender identity, as this includes transgender people, too).

I'm treating virginity here as more than an intact hymen inside the body of a girl or young woman. Energetically, the core of virginity in these contexts is as a gift of purity that the child embodies when given by the family to another. Throughout patriarchal history this has been about female hymens being undisturbed as a symbol of how honorable the family is, but it's about much more. The family is to spend a great deal of its energy over the life of the child focusing on creating one who is a gift to society or the world. Much of the time it has attached benefit for the family as regards finances, influence, politics, and/or status, but it's also about the family deriving a sense of worth from how pure and unstained their girl children turn out to be.

Regarding virginity, virtue, and worth, we're living in a time between two worlds. Many people are growing up in families that have either shed these old-timey norms or are finding it inevitable that they must. There's a lot of pain both in unmet expectations when the child expects to be taken care of and kept safe and when the father or family realizes that the child has not turned out to meet the proscribed expectations. When these expectations are not met and people are hurting from feeling let down by each other, what loyalty can remain? If it's been based on love and bonding, or what is thought of the strongest ties that are sourced in sharing blood, there's hope for healing. On the other hand, if it's been rooted in feeling safe if certain conditions are met and particular transactions performed, it might be harder to feel as if one belongs to those people who were supposed to make one feel safe and supported, or those who one believed would grow up to make you proud. Essentially, if the child bases his or her sense of being safe and someone who belongs on what the family members do or don't do, it might be a rocky path full of disappointment. The same goes for the family that bases its willingness to accept and support a child based on that child's behavior and choices.

And so what loyalty can a daughter have for a father or, in general, a child to a parent or family? Each person has to define what loyalty is to him or her, while also being responsible for the effort and time invested when loyalty is an issue. If loyalty grows from love, both parties have a chance to grow as they heal from the inevitable disappointments each will treat the other to as the child grows up into being his or her own person, beyond the control of the family and their long history of expectations who that child would turn out to be.

While it's daddy's job to cultivate the virtue of his own little girl, it might not stop him from being chemically activated by other little girls. The daughter will over time become acutely aware of this reality, noticing how he tries to cover his automatic responses to her peers or other young women. It may even be that while the father tries to keep himself in line, he can't help have such automatic responses to his own daughter. Incest and molestation are a couple of the ways that the daddy's little girl myth can veer into destructive, damaging territory, but it can also be damaging for the daughter to witness her father having feelings or urges regarding someone her own age or just a few years older. It makes it obvious that he isn't perfect (which no father is) but if he's spent time promising perfection if she herself delivers on his version of her perfection, this can be grounds for a painful rift. Inevitably, the daughter and her peers will develop sexually, and the myth of perpetual safety between them will be destroyed.

Thereby, the inevitable reality of sexuality becomes a most important and prevalent ground on which the daddy's little girl fantasy falls apart. Most daughters will develop into sexual beings and most fathers already are, and this is a reality that cannot be avoided. If the myth of mutual perfection resulting in safety for the daughter and allegiance and honor for the father is clung to—and healthy boundaries and allowance for the daughter to become her own kind of adult are put off—the warts on the loving connection between them can come to define the relationship, leaving both potentially feeling let down, unhappy, and hurt enough to be bitter toward and untrusting of the other. When a daddy's little girl scenario falls apart, each person can feel a sense of betrayal, leaving scars that can affect other interpersonal relationships.

Note the commonality of adults forming romantic/sexual relationships with others who remind them of one of their parents. Sometimes this is obvious right away, but more often it becomes obvious only after trust and various forms of intimacy are established, when the unprocessed wounding from childhood inevitably rises to the surface to be healed. The adult can't be fully present in any relationship until this is resolved, and the current partner perfectly stimulates the old pain. While it can be painfully uncomfortable and sometimes seeming too much to handle, these situations can be important vehicles for us to learn about what from our past hasn't yet been fully resolved and healed.

An End to Parthenogenesis

We began this chapter with a note about the mythology of Athene emerging fully formed from her father's head and, even, fully armored. The myth is a device to attempt to attribute Athene—including her wisdom, courage, strength, and accomplishments—to her father. The reason she came out of her father was that, upon hearing that one of his children would end up being the lord of heaven (and therefore supplanting him), Zeus swallowed Metis, Athene's then-pregnant mother. When the child was born, she was born inside her father. The patriarchal attempt to circumvent the mother in order to trick us into loyalty to the father is a blatant attempt to diminish the feminine, the central aspect of the heart of the patriarchal agenda to shift emphasis and positive sentiment only to the masculine in as many areas of life as possible.

But who does this goddess turn out to be? Athene proves herself through her wisdom, courage, and strength, tempering what she inherited from her father with, no doubt, what she inherited from her mother. As we live the stories of Pallas Athene, we can't choose to be blind to the fact that we are products of the lineages of each side of our family. We can't value the love of the father over that of the mother and still be aligned with love—we can't diminish one half of our true nature and still be or remain loving.

Whenever we may have found ourselves believing we needed to pledge allegiance to the father's agenda – or, more broadly, to a masculine agenda centered on control, direction, and shaping what naturally seeks healthy expression—we need to forgive ourselves. It's time to cease favoring the masculine over the feminine, but this includes coming into a more balanced state by refraining from judgment of where we've been and what we've believed to be right for so long. We as a collective have been playing that game in order to see what it's like, to find out what denying the value of half of our individual and collective true nature would feel like. But we're ready to be done with it, and we are already shifting out of the imbalance. The last few decades (since the first fists raised in the air in protest by the feminism of the early 1970s) have seen many of us decide that we're not going to live that way any longer and create change in our lives and the world around us. There's a wealth of pain to deal with, and shame and guilt, too, but things are changing.

The only escape from trying to force ourselves into an artificial parthenogenetic identity is to accept responsibility that, beyond childhood, no one should be expected to make us feel safe. Allegiance to the masculine agenda is based on the presumption by both parties that those pledging allegiance will be kept safe and secure, and will have nothing to worry about as long as they do what's expected of them. Daddy's little girl and related stories are mythological constructs that hide the archetypal reality that each and every human must grow into a separate, independent adulthood, becoming the source of love and support for the self. *True maturity isn't in passing the baton of who's in charge of protecting whom down through generations. It's in individuals maturing beyond the expectation that someone else will make them feel safe and secure, and will ensure their survival.*

Every soul has its human selves here to learn to, at first as infants and then children, rely upon others for everything and then grow into being self-sufficient. We often see this as expressed for many in terms of financial security, as the majority of us grow into being adults capable of supporting ourselves in the world in that way. But emotional and inner security have not for the most part been on the list of training modules we employ to show each other how to live as adults. It's a symptom of the collective fear that power is always misused and, since we can't trust ourselves to use it wisely, we clearly shouldn't be in charge of ourselves. The vast numbers of people in our world who do not feel safe in it (and, therefore, do not feel safe in their bodies, their homes, their relationships, and other places) evidence this. It can result in a lack of inner confidence that they can make the right choices for themselves, leading to the development of a populace unsure of who should be in charge of their lives. We're now living through an unwinding of the the idea that those nominally or functionally in charge of us and our society are qualified to be so, and are responsible enough to be entrusted with our safety and security.

And so what will we do in the face of this reality? If daddy's no longer qualified to be in charge, or if there's simply no daddy around, what are we to do? What's supposed to be happening? We are to take over working on behalf of our own highest good, relinquishing the perception that someone is supposed to be taking care of us. This is the path of spiritual maturity, wherein each of us steps up to be the source of strength and love for ourselves, letting everyone else off the hook, and getting over puerile fantasies that we should entrust our care and highest good to another.

Eris: Pushing Buttons and Lighting Fires

The story of Eris sets into motion the events that lead to the Trojan War, a major and defining event of the ancient world. In a way, though, it is easy to see the Trojan War only in terms of what was created as a result of it. Two great epic poems from antiquity each paint a version of it: *The Iliad* tells the story of the war and *The Odyssey* tells an absurdly long tale that begins at the end of the war. These two works are central to the Western canon, and all children in Western schools learn about at least some of the events and heroic and tragic happenings of this war. In mythological terms, the Trojan War serves as a backdrop for Western culture in several important ways.

For the purposes of this chapter, we'll focus here on the beginning of the war, the single act that started it, a single choice by a single individual.

Eris is the goddess of discord. Because of her tendency to bring it wherever she goes, she is not invited to the wedding of Peleus and Thetis on Mount Olympus. Honestly, would *you* want the goddess whose name means "strife" to come to your wedding? Chances are she'd ruin everything, right? Eris is, in fact, the only deity not invited; the rest of Olympus is going while she is intentionally excluded.

When she learns that she's not invited, she becomes enraged. She fashions or obtains a golden apple with the inscription "For the fairest" and tosses it into the middle of three goddesses at the reception—goddesses who have been invited—Aphrodite, Hera, and Athena. Each of the three goddesses thinks that the inscripted message is meant for her, and they argue over just who it is that's the fairest. Zeus is called upon to settle the conflict.

Now, because Zeus has been around the block a few zillion times, there's no way he is going to get in the middle of three goddesses in such an argument! He knows that whichever one he picks, he will have made one friend and two enemies. He is nothing if not an astute politician. Instead of settling the conflict as expected, he decides to appoint an impartial human to make the decision. Enter Paris. Zeus scours the nooks and crannies of the countryside to find the right guy and appoints the prince to make the decision.

Paris is then confronted with the choice of which Goddess is the fairest (see the next chapter, "Paris and the Power of Choice," for a full exploration of this).

Each goddess offers Paris a prize (ahem, a *bribe*) for choosing her. Paris picks Aphrodite, whose bribe was the offer of the most beautiful woman to be his bride, who happens to be one Helen of Troy, who happens already to be married. Aphrodite's sponsorship and wheel-greasing of the stealing away of Helen by Paris is the initial spark of the Trojan War and, well, the rest is history.

Buttons and Fires

Eris's role in this story concerns a single action that sets off a chain of events that changes everything for everyone involved and, in fact, changes the whole world.

This happens all of the time; it is inevitable. A single choice does not *often* result in grandiose cultural waveforms toppling over the globe such as life-changing wars but each major life-changing event can be traced to a single act by a single individual to push a button in or in some way light a fire under someone else—it is simply how life and the world work. You can talk about the strokes of butterfly wings here changing the course of events there and we can speak about the soul-level karmic contracts each of us has with other humans that play out over the courses of our lives but we, in fact, cannot live a life without being drawn into or caused to change. We might crave stability and for things to stay however they are but it simply cannot happen. Life changes us, and others are life's messengers for us as we are life's messengers for them.

In the end, it really doesn't matter what terms you use. The bottom line is that for change to happen someone must do something—push a button or light a fire—and the change that results is not just inevitable but necessary.

From the vantage point of soul, all that happens to us teaches us what it is like to be incarnated here, which is what souls come here to learn. All that happens in our lives serves to educate us about what we need to learn—even the difficult things. Everything that happens to you causes you to make a decision or refuse to do so, which is just another kind of decision. Each experience you have changes you, and change is the name of the game. There can be no progress (growth) without it. Eris's role as we live her story in our lives is to instigate change even when other parties do not want to change and, often, are not aware of precisely what's going on. Her role is to introduce a little chaos, discord, and strife to get the ball rolling in all kinds of situations and dynamics in our lives.

In terms of the mythological story, the truth to be seen through our spiritual eyes (beyond our human eyes, or from a bird's-eye view that encompasses why we experience what we do) is that all fear must in time be confronted, seen, and worked through, transmuted, and released. Holding onto fear keeps us from growing, and the natural course of things—the natural course of our soul's journey over our many human lives—calls for all fears to be explored and dealt with. The ideal outcome is that we overcome the fear, which then leads to healing and/or releasing pain garnered from past experiences and related to what is feared. It is never in our best interests to perpetuate fear, and we in our psychological sophistication can probably all agree it is never healthy. Facing and processing fear is one part of empowerment we experience as spirit having human experiences and, in a way, our entire lives can be seen as opportunities to confront, heal, and transmute fear into self-empowerment.

In the myth, the insecurities of each of the three goddesses need to be triggered. They cannot learn to deal with these insecurities and heal past pain related to their fears if the insecurities remain hidden. Eris in this story, it turns out, is a very valuable teacher for Aphrodite, Hera, and Athena. She stirs things up and gives them the opportunity to figure out how to grow out of limiting circumstances that, truth be told, probably limit the goddesses' expression and experience in important ways. What they do with these opportunities is up to them, of course, but such triggers are important for our growth processes, and Eris is the one to bring them.

Eris isn't just blindly making a decision, though, to toss some old golden apple into the middle of a party. It isn't that she's simply throwing a thing into a place, ignorant of the effect her action might have; she is acutely aware of the insecurities of those present. In her anger from being rejected, she is intentionally bringing their insecurities to light. *It is her wish to push the buttons of those among whom she feels overlooked.* She feels dissed and she's going to lash out, and she knows the best way to do this is to let them fight amongst themselves, to sow discord, and then to let everyone else do the heavy lifting of engendering conflict and manifesting the unhappiness of strife. She knows that she has to do just one mere thing, a simple little thing that might set them off, and then she can get out of the way and enjoy the fruits of their fears being triggered.

In Our Day-to-Day Lives

As we live Eris's story in our day-to-day lives, it has much to do with pushing buttons and lighting fires when it comes to other people—whether we know we are doing it or not, whether they know we are doing it or not, and whether anyone involved *likes* it or not. We often do not have any idea that we are doing this yet, when hurt, we can figure out how to manipulate circumstances in order to maximize the suffering of those who have hurt us.

Each person has insecurities. Some of us experience them our entire lives and do not ever learn to deal with, heal, or put them in context in order to cease being deeply hurt when they are brought to light and others see them. Eris people serve the rest of us by making it impossible to ignore the fears that we carry, no matter our relationship with those fears and no matter our intentions regarding them (whether we want to deal with them or not).

You can probably think of numerous examples in your life when you or someone around you capitalized on someone else's insecurity in order to cut them down, elicit revenge, or generally just make someone else's life unpleasant for some reason. We're not all monsters all the time; we all have sensitive hearts and the capability to sense into what is happening with others. So when we do this it doesn't make us "bad" people, per se—it simply means we are wounded people who choose to lash out sometimes.

You can probably see Eris in yourself in at least one part of your life. Think back to your younger school days. If someone wasn't criticizing or picking on you, you might have feared that they or someone else might. Remember how you were able to pick up on that person's insecurities and how you thought about using them against the person? Whether you acted on it or not, you were living an Eris story. Responding to pain (and please remember that all anger is rooted in pain) by wanting to hurt another person is living an Eris story—even if you don't follow through on it and begin some sort of Trojan War (scale being relative, of course).

Eris's own insecurities have to do with being accepted. Why else would she react so strongly to not being invited? She does not react because she is the only goddess who was not invited. It is not the logic of the situation or an objective, egalitarian sensibility having been wronged that triggers her; it is her fear of rejection and loneliness. She reacts as she does because she is hurt. And when her fear becomes manifest she lashes out from her pain.

This latter bit is not in the myth. This is one point at which it becomes important to separate the myth that we have received from the archetypal process as we live it. We have to understand that Eris has feelings. We can know this because *we* have feelings and the gods and goddesses of mythology are within us. We can therefore put ourselves in her place and see that her reaction is rooted in her *own* insecurities. It can be easy to view through unsympathetic eyes someone who chooses to hurt or lash out at another after being caused pain. Yet I feel strongly that one of the major teachings to come from the archetype of Eris as she enters our collective vocabulary in the early 21st century is to teach us that all anger is rooted in pain.

Another facet of this myth as social instruction that needs to be made clear is that it supports the culturally manufactured idea that women need to be in competition with each other for beauty, which gets translated into acceptance (which is, of course, actually love). "Beauty deserves love" is one idealized cultural teaching related to this myth (while "difficult women do not deserve love" could be another). Somewhere along the way we have, on one level, bought into the idea that more beauty is deserving of more love, which is one reason youth is valued so strongly in our culture and those who are aging are valued less and less as they age. Our standard of beauty is tied to idealized youth and, for the brief window of time a human fits the ideal, he or she is valued in unconscious ways by those who have absorbed this cultural meme.

In the part of the story in which the three goddesses argue over who is the fairest, it is easy to see the angle of competition. But this competition is also why Eris is so hurt and angry that she is excluded from the big party. Eris is the goddess of discord—when she brings it with her (which she does everywhere she goes), she is not loved. It is her true nature to be who she is, and she does not receive love as a result of expressing it. She looks around at what it seems to take to get love (beauty), and though she may be beautiful,[7] she also comes with seeds of strife and discord that make just about all around her unhappy (and, remember, maybe difficult women do not deserve love). It is simply the effect that she has on others; it is the signature that she carries.

The cultural deal with competition between women for beauty (and, therefore, love) is an artificial mechanism meant to distract women from learning what true empowerment is and then embodying it. It is artifice and a glamour, which is to say illusory and not based in truth. It is part of the patriarchal mission to diminish the feminine in order to maintain a focus on the priorities of the chosen masculine agenda.[8] The short of it is that if women

---

[7] I've found no reference to whether Eris is considered beautiful or not.

[8] See *Living Myth: Exploring Archetypal Journeys* for more on this idea as well as a chapter on each on two of the goddesses involved in the fight for the apple, Athena (as Pallas Athene)

are catty and in competition with each other, they will never have time or energy to figure out how to support and help each other come to and embody a healthy and grounded version of feminine strength in the at-present severely imbalanced cultural context in which we live. It's a divide-and-conquer thing with a heaping dose of perpetuated disempowerment thrown in. While many women do support each other and form networks of cooperation of various kinds and have *always* done so, my focus here is on the cultural transmission for which the myth is a vehicle because of the widespread impact the story has had on how people live. And it is true that the reach of these cultural teachings is far and wide in the psyches and hearts of many.

Eris's story is not one widely told at this point in time for it is not a popular myth. As a matter of fact, the only reason I am aware of it is because of the dwarf planet identified and named Eris that is beginning to be used in astrological circles.[9] As we begin to tell this story to each other, we must be

---

and Hera (as Juno). See *Goddess Past, Present, and Future* for a channeled perspective on the history of the patriarchy and the diminishment of the feminine. Lastly, *Lilith: Healing the Wild* covers the development of the patriarchy and how to dismantle it through the Lilith archetype.

[9] First seen in 2003, officially recognized in 2005, named Eris in 2006.

aware of how we word it and what we weave and thread into it as the moral message. Since all myths support someone's intellectual, philosophical, and/or moral agenda, we have to remember to see beyond the angle of competition or of competition between women (or pettiness and insecurities) and understand it on deeper levels.

Cycles of Pain

When we live Eris stories, we believe that sowing the seeds of pain in another person will somehow, in some way, make us feel better. Of course, it will not. It *cannot*, in fact—no matter what we do to act out the pain, including bringing pain to others. The vast majority of us knows the following the vast majority of the time: *Responding to pain by doling out pain to others merely creates a cycle of suffering and, in some situations, abuse.* Yet in those moments of despair when our innermost fears and insecurities have been exposed for all to see, when we feel our emotional nerves and innards exposed to the open air, we need to believe that there is some remedy for our pain. Oh, and look over there—*that's* who caused it! So it is natural when we see these situations through our human eyes (when someone seems to be acting upon us, when we do not grasp that we are experiencing something of our own soul's creation) to blame others and want to do something about it *to* them so that they suffer.

The highest use of pain as a teacher for us is to learn the importance of choosing compassion in the face of pain of self and other. The fact is that we get hurt. It happens. It is a normal part of standard human experience and there isn't a human who does not experience it. Anyone who believes that it is not normal and part of the human journey is still in an infantile mode of seeking security outside the self and expecting others or the world to provide it. Spiritually mature people tap into the fact that all that happens to us supports us in learning the lessons our soul has come to Earth to learn. Yet in the moment of being hurt, even the best or most evolved of us can slip into a "poor me" stance, from within which it can look like someone else has done something to us—a victim stance. We cannot all always in those moments grasp that we have cocreated the scenario, the reason we would have done it, and what we are supposed to be learning through the experience.

Choosing compassion in the face of pain and suffering is the only way out of pain and suffering. Period.

Eris's story can remind us of the important truth that all anger is sourced in pain. She does what she does because she has been snubbed. Similarly, *we* may be motivated to cause others pain because *we* have been hurt. Remembering that all anger is sourced or rooted in pain, we can easily see that compassion is the route to preventing things like Trojan Wars in our lives and the lives of others (scales, of course, being relative).

What's My Motivation?

Given that we are sometimes living Eris's story in our lives—that we will sometimes trigger other people even when we and they are not aware of what is happening—we have the choice about *why* we do it. Each of us can at all times choose the motivation behind our triggering of other people and if we are going to be doing it, let's just get clear already about why it's going to happen.

I have the energy of Eris strong in my life. I have a deep sensitivity to the insecurities of others and often seem to show up as a trigger or catalyst for people. When it comes to Eris, *catalyst* is a fantastic word; however, it implies that there is a positive intended end, which the person on the other end of the catalyzing can't always see clearly after being triggered.

Before I began the astrological and spiritual counseling work I do now, I was hesitant to bring this part of me out. It always seems to make others uncomfortable, and I didn't want to make things harder for other people.[10] Now I can see the value in pushing other people's buttons and in lighting fires under them. Through my work, people come to me to learn about the unseen parts of themselves, to burrow down into the source of their fears and dilemmas, and I help them see how to work with and release them. The work I do, in other words, is a perfect arena for bringing the energy of Eris to others. My agreement with myself about this part of me includes that I only do it consciously and intentionally *when asked* to do it—you book a session with me and I'm all yours. But if I'm out socially, my radar for others' insecurities is not active. Most of the time when a client comes in to see me, he or she is aware that I can see deeply into things. It is important for me to honor client boundaries, making myself available to trigger and catalyze their processes when they are open and ready to receive it, and it's important that I myself have boundaries and use this part of me only when it is appropriate and welcome.

---

[10] The year after I began seeing clients, after one of my dearest friends had sampled my work, he suggested (humorously, of course) that I add a brief warning to my business card: "Making things harder for people since 2003."

I do this deep seeing, however, with a loving motivation: I make myself available for this and only to serve the highest good of everyone involved. This is a critical point, the centerpiece of the entire chapter. It is the key point about the energy of Eris within us that will need to be a cornerstone for how we move forward in our exploration of and dialogue about her in our lives.

For anyone with a strong Eris energy (and you will know if you are one by this point in the chapter, though you can also look her up in your astrological birth chart[11]), motivation is everything. Such people will trigger others. No doubt about it and nothing to do for it. The reason for doing it (what is in their hearts prior to and as they do it) will determine if growth and healing or discord and strife are triggered. Another who finds him- or herself triggered will look to the person bringing the trigger for signs and hints of malice and the will to harm,

---

[11] Visit www.astro.com to generate your own birth chart. Because of Eris's long orbital period relative to other elements used widely in astrology, some say that Eris is not important on a personal level. It has been transiting full-time in Aries since late 1926, so almost all humans on the planet as of this writing in 2017 have the dwarf planet in Aries. I argue that the fact that most of us have it in Aries means that we are attempting to work through similar themes together—not that the individual placement is less important because we all have it in the same sign.

and so embodying compassion for others (because it is true that we all have insecurities) is the surest route to navigating Eris stories in positive ways.

An important point to discuss regarding how we live the energy of Eris is that as the goddess of discord, whose name means "strife," the initial effect on others by an Eris person can be very difficult. We're talking about deep fears and insecurities being highlighted and pressed on, after all, which can include the dredging of psychic and emotional sewers that can catch a person off-guard. Most of us usually don't want to look at our fears and so we bury and stuff them. When the Eris person comes along and those nerves get exposed, it can be very difficult to appreciate the influence that person has on us as a teacher, as a catalyst to growth, by making our secret fears and insecurities plain. We learn to appreciate such people and the wakes they leave in our lives, but often only in retrospect. Many times, in fact, this happens decades after they have left our lives.

But it *is* possible to appreciate Eris's button-pushing in the moment. If we can understand the spiritual principle that others show up to teach us what we need to learn and that we are energetically complicit in the situation—that we as energetic beings ask to be taught by vibrating in our energy fields a need to learn something—we can maintain the bird's-eye view that often comes from retrospection years after the dust has settled. The question then becomes if we can remain grounded enough in this spiritual principle to observe with conscious awareness what is happening when an Eris person shows up in our lives. "Remain grounded" here means to feel what we are feeling but be stable enough and rooted in the spiritual truth mentioned above to be able to stay focused on what is really happening. For better or worse, we are prone to being swept away by our emotions. Getting grounded in some sort of truth and thereby being able to remain in our bodies leaves us able to deal with the feelings that we have instead of being knocked off-course or derailed by their depth and intensity. The space that Eris figures open in us can leave us feeling raw and uncontrolled, and wanting to act accordingly, and so it is imperative that we learn to stay grounded and in our hearts, bodies, and minds to deal with the situation in front of us.

The other side of this is when *we* show up as the Eris figure. Can we remain grounded enough in the truth of cocreation and in the truth that the teacher appears when we need to learn a lesson, so that we can refrain from taking sole (and guilt-inspiring) responsibility for another's pain? Can we allow ourselves to trigger someone else into his or her pain—which is a necessary process on that person's path to growth—and not choose to feel shame or guilt for it?

As pain is a necessary part of the human journey, we need to learn to understand its place in our lives. When we choose to deal with pain rather than run away from it, we always end up better off. Many of us, as mentioned above, are looking for safety, security, and protection, a frankly infantile dreamscape in which we believe nothing can hurt us. In this kind of place, someone is protecting us so that if something *did* try to hurt us, it would not be able to. It sounds great to a lot of people, but it neither supports nor leads to spiritual maturity. Collectively we are coming out of a long phase of believing that someone is going to take care of us, a sort of spiritual adolescence. We are moving into a more self-aware state of understanding that energy is the root of everything, and that we are in charge of our energies and all that happens to us. We are beginning to learn that we are making all of this happen, and waking up to learning to manage it more intentionally.

While the myth of Eris has been around a long time, the planetary body with this name was given it in the year 2006. When a planetary body of any kind is named, it is time for that archetype to come into collective consciousness. It is time for the energy to be understood as *part* of us, and it is time for us to begin discussing and processing it and its apparent lessons.

A true understanding of the lessons and invitations of the energy of Eris await us as we explore the use and point of pain and suffering, the value of change and those who help us change (even when we hate doing it and feel tortured by it), and the truth about the responsibilities we have to ourselves and to others. Grasping the value of triggering others' fears in the service of their (needed and inevitable) growth will take us into a healthy and grounded relationship with the energy of discord and strife, allowing us to support each other in our individual and collective evolution.

As awareness of Eris finds its way in the collective consciousness, we have the choice to explore what it means to take responsibility for all that happens to us. As this archetype emerges into full light within our fields and we can see it active in our lives, we have the opportunity to view others as triggers and to withdraw the expectation that they take responsibility for what we experience. It will be tempting to view others as the sources of our pain, to be sure. Will we choose to see in the moment of its unfolding the importance of growth? Can we become willing to experience our deep pain coming to the surface and choose to see the moment as an opportunity to heal something we couldn't have become conscious of on our own? Will we choose to thank our most important teachers, those who have pushed our buttons repeatedly and lit fires under us at times when we felt we could least take it?

Paris and the Power of Choice

Now that we've looked at Eris's part of the story, let's look at that of Paris. He is faced with favoring one goddess over two others in the famed "Judgment of Paris." I am not sure Paris knows that the two he does not choose will become his enemies, though this was clear enough to Zeus, the one who refused to make the choice and roped the innocent and naïve ~~schlep~~ shepherd into the situation. Initially Paris comes through to me as a simple person just waiting to be plucked to be someone's patsy, but there is more going on here.

He is thrust into the limelight when slated to choose the most beautiful from among the three goddesses re the golden apple business. He is launched into what must be for him a terrifying and exciting new experience. And whichever goddess he chooses, he knows during his deliberation, he will be a very different person on the other side. He doesn't know precisely how he'll change, but he can sense that this is big.

I see this as akin to the limelight some people on reality television are thrown into. Often there is no unique talent or specialized skill that warrants their inclusion or selection. They might be chosen for a show precisely because they are regular people, because producers and network types know the viewers will be able to relate to them. Paris was chosen because Zeus did not want to incur the wrath of the two goddesses he would not have chosen. Paris is being used by Zeus just as the producers of reality television are using those on the shows, though of course in a slightly different way. The effect on each participant, however, is the same after being thrust into the limelight for his or her fifteen minutes of fame.

I'm thinking specifically of the shows where one man or woman has over the course of weeks to evaluate and pick one of dozens of the opposite sex, who are all hoping to be picked. They are on the show because they want that one person to choose them. So much personal stuff from the lives of all is exposed, especially the one person who will choose a date or mate or plaything from the dozens of options at the end of the show's season. Everything that is going on in that one person's process is laid bare for all of us to see, and this is what it was like for Paris as

88

he had to choose the fairest from among the three goddesses.

The myth tells us that Zeus chose Paris because he had recently displayed an uncommon sense of fairness in another situation. Again, I tend to initially read Paris as naïve and innocent, with not so much in the brains department. The stories that come down to us, however, are that he stands out for his intelligence. Paris is in fact a Trojan, the son of royal parents Priam and Hecuba. Prior to his birth, his mother had a dream a seer interpreted to mean that Paris would grow up to be the fall of Troy. After he was born, he was to be killed so he could not be the cause of its end, yet no one appointed the task could kill him. He ended up being cared for and raised by a shepherd far away from where he had been born. So he has grown up in obscurity, and is now chosen for this very important task ... that is in fact *not* that important, but everyone thinks it is, perhaps because of the human susceptibility to be swept away in meaningless PR stunts and the dramas of the gods and goddesses.

Prizes

Each goddess offers Paris what is called a prize for choosing her, though they are bribes. (It's not only Zeus who is politically astute.) Aphrodite offers Paris the most beautiful woman in the world to be his bride. Hera offers him ownership of Europe and Asia. Athena offers wisdom or skill in battle (depending on the source).

Imagine being offered the chance to choose from among such options. Paris is not really choosing the goddess who is the most fair—he is choosing which bribe he wants. (Paris is not politically astute.) He is simply a young man without much worldly experience, given the option to choose between three pretty much unbelievable and superlative door prizes any old ~~schlep~~ shepherd would be thrilled to have. He ends up choosing the most beautiful woman in the world as his prize, which is to say that he chooses Aphrodite as the fairest of the three goddesses. She lets him know that Helen, Queen of Sparta, is the woman he will have, and she helps him in several ways to accomplish the difficult task of stealing her away from her husband, with whom she has been happy and who is not in the least interested in letting her go. The result of the cuckolded King Menelaus's anger and pain is the Trojan War.

On one level, the story a moral warning to make major decisions with some part of you that is not wired to your genitals, or not to choose from lust.

When Paris does choose this way,[12] the result is a fantastically gigantic war the likes of which no one had ever seen. We are supposed to choose with some other part of ourselves—we are supposed to reason, to consider consequences, to think. We are supposed to use our heads and look before we leap. The underlying current of moralizing here tells us that lust is reckless and never gets us to good places. We are to choose with our reasoning faculties because, the reasoning mind insists, it doesn't get us into nearly as much trouble (though it of course can, the cultural investment here is to get us into our brains and not give sway to our hormones).

Choice is Power

Let's go back to who Paris really is. He is the son of a king and queen, a prince of Troy. He is noble by birth yet living in obscurity as a shepherd. When he is appointed judge in the contest between the three goddesses, he is pretty much a nobody in the eyes of all but, presumably, his adoptive parents and their sheep.

As we live Paris's story in our daily lives, we are almost never thrust into the limelight to make major

---

[12] This or because he is drawn in by the promise of ideal beauty in manifest form being his to have and hold. Either way, he is not in any way thinking clearly.

choices with undeniable consequences that end up changing everything. Infrequently is a choice waiting for us to make with such far-reaching consequences as Paris's, one that ends in something as serious and important as the Trojan War.

Yet as modern people seeking to develop spiritual sophistication, we need to understand that each choice we make is in fact an act of divine power. We are divine creative beings yet have, in our quest to learn about being human, forgotten it. In many ways the soul's journey through its many human lives is one of remembering just how powerful we are with our creative energies.[13] We are learning that everything in our lives is a manifestation of what we vibrate, both consciously and unconsciously.[14]

Paris is noble by birth yet living in obscurity as a shepherd. He has no idea who he really is, or was meant to be. We are divine creators by birth and are living in obscurity as whatever we think we are, which is usually shaped by the kind of people and places we come from and what we do in the world, often meaning our jobs. We, like Paris, have no idea about who we really are.

---

[13] See *The Soul's Journey I* for more on this.
[14] See *Conscious Revolution: Tools for 2012 and Beyond* for channeled perspectives on the manifestation process.

Paris's choice is a sort of cartoony extreme of what we do all the time. We are confronted with making a choice and, often, we know that what we choose will change things. Choosing one thing often cuts off the possibility of what is not chosen, and perhaps other things that were related to it or might stem from it. We make peace with this reality as we grow up and age, as we navigate the realities of creating a life for ourselves as we go.

There is much juice at this time in our evolution to get inside and deeply grasp what it means to choose, as well as understand how each choice is an act of creative power. Many are waking up to the truth that each thing we do generates and emits energy. We are just beginning to learn that whatever frequency we are running when we make a choice contributes to creating the world around us. This is the source of the stuff you've heard about how important it is to think positive thoughts and so on. It is also the basis for new age teachings such as "The Secret" that take this old wisdom and reframe it for new age ears and minds. What you are thinking and feeling and believing is creating your reality, these teachings tell us. They ask us what kind of reality we wish to live in, and invite us to change our thoughts in order to make it happen.

There are two frequencies down to which every energy, thought, feeling, and motivation can be reduced: faith and fear. (Faith can also be called love.) When you make a choice based in faith, you create the energy of faith around you and are sowing something positive. When you choose based in fear, you sow the energy of fear around you and are sowing something not positive. Faith leads to more faith and fear leads to more fear. Whichever motivation you choose, you broadcast the frequency of it and it is this creates the world around you. It creates more and more of it in your life going forward.

What I have been shown about the opportunities being presented to us now is in large part about gaining conscious awareness of the difference between choosing from faith and fear, and then learning to do whatever it takes to get from choosing from fear or from both in a back-and-forth fashion to choosing from faith. Such a transition in my experience involves doing much emotional healing in order to be more present to what is going on in the moment in front of us.[15]

In the context of this story of Paris, we are all the time faced with choices that, once made, will change

---

[15] See *The Soul's Journey I* for more on this.

things. The question to ask ourselves is how aware of and in touch we are with our motivation for making whatever choice we make. We can know with certainty that we will be confronted with the task of making choices—it is a fact of life. And we know that we will have to decide in one direction or another, and we also have gotten wise to the truth that refusing to make a choice between two options is in fact also making a choice. But in the end, it turns out that what we choose in any given situation is not nearly as important as *why* we choose it.

When looking at what it is that we want to create with and through our lives, our motivation is everything. *Motivation creates a state of being, no matter what specific thing is chosen with and through that motivation.* This is critical to those who want to change things in their life for the better.

Do you know people who are afraid to make choices? I do. I've been one of them at times. You might have been one, too. Sometimes we are afraid because choosing one possibility is necessarily limiting. We know that choosing one fork in the road means that we will not get to go down the other. When we are in this situation we need to become aware of the fact that because we are afraid to let go of the other possibility, we will never enjoy or be able to inhabit the one we do end up choosing. At other times we might fear choosing because then something is going to happen, and we will be the ones responsible for it. Sometimes this fear keeps us dancing with potential outcomes and futures in ways that keep us from having to appear to ourselves responsible for what's happening in our lives.

You might also know people who put off deciding, or who refuse to make choices. Each of these is also a choice and an act of creative power. When we do not choose we keep away from ourselves the effect of all of the possibilities in front of us in a given situation. We also make the choice to let the universe, life, the world, or whatever outside force works for your vocabulary and viewpoint to make choices for us. Things around us will always shift and change, even if we refuse to change with them. When we do this, in time we will find ourselves in scenarios when the choice we refused to make will have been made for us, and we will feel pressed into it against our will. This can be difficult. It can also reinforce the feeling of powerlessness of which a refusal to choose is always evidence.

Awareness and Time
Since each choice is an act of power, each one needs to be made with conscious awareness. When we are inclined to hesitate, we are better off to take

our time to figure out what we are afraid of before making the choice. We also need to let go of judgments we have about certain kinds of choices. This story about Paris in part teaches us to steer clear of making choices with our hot-to-trot chemical selves or idealistic selves. Yet there are times in life when those parts are the ones that have all the information we need, and we actually need to run with what they say and want. There is, for example, a biological imperative that comes into play at times and it is healthy to let go of judgment when it makes itself known. I recently heard a woman begin her life story with an acknowledgement that her parents had little to do with each other after she was conceived. She accepted that the imperative to come together (karma is often the main fuel for the chemistry when such relationships form and break up quickly) had to do with bringing her into this life.

Conversely, there are times when our chemical parts weigh in as a reflection of something else. One example is when we seek pleasure in lieu of something else that we perceive we cannot get. A specific example in this context would be someone who seeks sexual gratification because he or she feels unable to meet an emotional need. The point is that being clear about our motivations for making choices is more important than we have so far really understood.

This carries over into all areas of life. Why do we eat what we eat? Why are these particular people our friends, lovers, or spouses? Why do we do the work we do? Why do we work where we do? Why do we pursue the hobbies we do? Ask yourself what you think you are getting by making those choices, and then ask yourself what you are *in fact* getting from them. Odds are that you will learn a ton about yourself you didn't even know was waiting for you to learn.

So, yes, choice changes things, but really everything. I think I'll end this chapter with some questions for you.

What do you want to change? What are you willing to change?

Are you honest with yourself about what you don't want to or are unwilling to change?

Do you know why you choose what you choose?

Look at choices you make that you know are from faith. What tends to result from them? How often do you let these results inform how you choose next?

Look at choices you make that you know are rooted in fear. What usually results from them? How often do you let these result inform how you choose next?

What kinds of motivations in yourself do you judge? What kinds of responses to challenges (stirrings to choose) do you judge?

What kinds of motivations in others do you judge?

Are you willing to let go of your judgments and treat everything you could choose as a possible route to getting where you want to go?

Are you willing to give yourself a chance to be a work in progress and make the best possible choices? Are you willing to let yourself evolve through learning from the results of your choices?

Iphigenia's Sacrifice

The name of this mythological figure might not be on the tip of your tongue, let alone her story. We do however frequently find ourselves living Iphigenia's story and it appeared to me as a rich exploration of certain kinds of parent-child dynamics.

The Story

In the Greek tradition, Iphigenia is a good daughter to Agamemnon, King of Mycenae. Agamemnon's brother Menelaus (the king of Sparta) was married to Helen at the time that Paris whisked her off her feet with Aphrodite's help after the famed golden apple fiasco covered above. The Greek kingdoms united to avenge the wrong done to Menelaus and amassed their combined forces for two years before sailing for Troy for this act of vengeance we now call the Trojan War.

During this two-year period, Agamemnon happened to kill a stag that was sacred to Diana, goddess of the hunt. Diana visited upon the troops disease and calmed the winds so the ships could not sail. To remedy the wrong done to her, a soothsayer relayed that she demanded the sacrifice on her altar of a virgin, but only the virgin daughter of the man who killed the stag would do.

Enter Iphigenia.

This incredible and jaw-dropping armada, the largest ever assembled on Earth, is finally amassed. And after two years. it is finally ready to sail to war and its leader goes and ruins everything by killing the wrong forest creature. Oh, but he can fix it by sacrificing his daughter, who is minding her own business and has nothing to do with this impending war save for just happening to be the daughter of the man who stepped forward to lead it.

We are told that Agamemnon doesn't feel good about complying, but that he does. He calls for Iphigenia with the message that she is to come to meet him, as she will be wedded to Achilles, the great Greek hero. She comes as requested, but wait a minute! There's an altar on which she is to be sacrificed. At the very last second before the death blow is dealt, Diana changes her mind: She swoops in and replaces Iphigenia with a deer, removing the young woman and making her a priestess in Diana's temple.

Parental Sacrifice of a Child

Agamemnon's willingness to sacrifice Iphigenia speaks to his commitment to his goal, which is a goal shared with his united countrymen. They feel a great wrong has been perpetrated by a Trojan and it must be dealt with. The amassed military forces are a symbol of Greek pride and evidence of the united kingdoms' impressive strength. Something very big is happening here at Aulis, and to have it derailed or sabotaged by something like killing the wrong deer on a hunt is practically unthinkable, especially as it is the leader of the forces who has brought the wrath of Diana upon them.

Agamemnon knows he is responsible for his actions and I have little doubt that he would be willing to take responsibility for them by paying just about whatever price Diana demanded.[16] Yet when the soothsayer communicates that the goddess will be appeased with the sacrifice of his daughter and by this only, he accepts. He does not appeal to Diana via any means. He does not cry out at the injustice of it all and to offer himself instead of his daughter. I'm

---

[16] Except, I suspect, the ending or taking of his own life. Agamemnon is running on the fuel of vengeance, to right the wrong done to his brother Menelaus. Agamemnon cannot prove himself and his moral imperative the be-all, end-all if he is not alive to lead the armies against Troy.

not even sure it occurs to him to ask or to attempt to negotiate with the goddess or offer himself (not that she would have been willing to deal with him, but he could have tried! We want him as a parent to at least try).

If this looks to you like Agamemnon does not love Iphigenia, look more closely. He does love and appreciate her. He has however been for two years caught up in what we could call patriotic fervor surrounding the whole vengeance-on-Troy situation. He is also the chosen leader of the military campaign that is about to be launched against the city across the sea. It is also his brother who is the wronged party, around whom this entire situation has been revolving since day one. Agamemnon is therefore not thinking exactly straight. He is willing to sacrifice himself to right this wrong, and we see that he is also willing to sacrifice his daughter. In that moment, he values the shared national goal he has adopted and shared national pride he feels more than Iphigenia. Get a bunch of war-hungry people together and have them beat their chests for a couple of years as they become ridiculously heavily armed, salivating at the prospect of taking revenge for a wrong done to them, and see how clearly they end up thinking. The entire project, the whole reason all of them are at Aulis, is the pursuit of a puffed-up revenge fantasy, a bloodlust assumed to be heroic because of their particular moral issues about wife stealing. When we are fueled by a desire for revenge, we simply cannot think clearly, and this is the space in which we find Agamemnon.

But his daughter is not his to sacrifice. Perhaps it could be argued that in those days children belonged to their parents, at least girls who were not yet married off to belong to some other man. Viewing this through the lens of spiritual truth, however, tells us that he does not have the right to use his daughter in this way, and this will be important when we look in a moment at how we live this story in our own lives. We each have free will and are responsible for ourselves. In line with this, we want Agamemnon to appeal to Diana to allow him to repay the debt of the slain stag. We want him to insist that since he is the one who transgressed the goddess, that he should be the one who pays the price.

Sacrificing your own daughter is a horrible price to pay. But Iphigenia has nothing to do with this, with any of it. She is involved only because she is his daughter.

Diana taking pity on Iphigenia and replacing her with the deer at the last minute could be seen as an testament to her compassionate nature. I infer from this that she might have been willing to work with

Agamemnon to focus the punishment or payment more directly on him. I believe that since nothing here in fact had to do with Iphigenia, Diana would have no reason to actually punish her and/or not treat her well. Diana, after all, makes Iphigenia a priestess in her temple in the end, which she would not have done if Iphigenia had anything to do with the problem Agamemnon had created.

Iphigenia's Sacrifice in Our Lives

When we look at this story from the literal angle of "throwing your kid under the bus," we know it is not a widespread phenomenon. Yet when we zoom out just a bit by expanding how we define the word "sacrifice," we can see it in play in many parent-child relationships.

We sacrifice when we give up something important in the service of a larger, important goal or purpose. At times we sacrifice for an ideal or belief. At other times it is for a concrete goal, the importance of which outweighs what we are giving up. There are times when sacrifice is painless and others when it is very painful. The idea always is that we must give up one thing to create, enable, maintain, or further another.

Parents sacrifice for their children all the time. They give up things important to them in order to ensure the health, well-being, and happiness of the child. Many would say that parenthood is sort of all about sacrifice. What most parents sacrifice, however, is theirs to give up, and this is where as we live Iphigenia's story things get interesting.

In this story, a parent sacrifices something that belongs to the child. With Iphigenia it is the promise of a long, rich, full life. We can assume as the daughter of a king she would go on to live an at least somewhat interesting and fulfilling life (as much as a woman who was likely destined to be valued akin to cattle and traded for political and economic clout could). In killing her on the altar of Diana, Agamemnon would be taking away her literal life. As we live the story, it is more often future possibility and our capacity to believe in possibilities for ourselves that are on the altar under the hand of the parent.

Attitudes that are handed down through families is one category of vehicle for how we live this story. A family with definite political or social opinions can in its training of its young sacrifice the child's ability to see a larger picture. Racism and bigotry also come to mind as attitudes and beliefs that become instilled in children in some families. *People with this color skin or this kind of background are like this* if heard early and often enough goes a long way toward coloring a child's perceptions of the world. The same goes with commentary on social policy and the politics of the day. *Republicans are narrow-minded and are ruining this country* and *Democrats are idiots and are ruining this country* are two sorts of examples from this sphere.

Yet it carries over into attitudes of many kinds. Ideas about what it means when someone has a lot of money or very little money count, as do attitudes about living in various parts of town, parts of the country, or parts of the globe, not to mention prejudices and attitudes toward religions and people who believe things different than the family does. When we have such attitudes instilled in us, our view necessarily gets smaller. Our capacity to be open to experience is shaped and guided by these beliefs and we can, through believing them, limit the experiences we are open to finding waiting for us in the world. When we have experienced this in youth and then when older have consciously worked to undo them, it is hard work to unravel the knee-jerk reactions we have to certain kinds of topics and people. This sort of imprinting by our families can run deep.

The sacrifice here is of the child's sense of wonder at exploring the surrounding world. Question: *What are other people like?* Answer: *Those people are dirty and lie, those other ones cheat and steal.* Ok, question answered, right? The more we absorb from our families about what the world or those other people are like, the more we sacrifice actually finding out, which is often an amazing experience and can change our lives in ways no one can ever foresee.

There is also a thread to Iphigenia's story in play when a child lives in the shadow of the misery, grief, anger, or other persistent or dominating emotion of a parent. If a parent cannot deal with his or her emotion, it can take over a household, infecting all who live in it and coloring everything that goes on in it. A child with a parent experiencing unprocessed grief, for example, will come to be sensitive to triggering that parent to avoid stirring up the pot of unprocessed grief. Same goes with anger and misery. With these, nothing else bad can happen because the parent is already at the brink of something unhealthy or dangerous, and the child learns that making things worse must be avoided at all costs. What is sacrificed in these scenarios is the ability to feel safe in one's environment and to naturally feel and express the full range of human emotion. And it is usually inadvertent on the parent's part. He or she does not want to stifle the child, but simply cannot see how to work through the feelings in healthy ways that are self-responsible and do not involve the child. It is even clear to many that the emotions they carry that are shaping their kids have nothing to do with the kids, as Agamemnon's problem that needed fixing had in truth nothing to do with Iphigenia.

Going further with the example of misery, I have seen too often in my brief years on Earth parent-adult child relationships that are somehow centered on the parent insisting on being miserable and the adult child playing along. In our sophisticated present-day psychological lingo we see this is a form of codependency or enabling, yet looking at it through the lens of Iphigenia's story we can see it as some goal of a parent calling for sacrifice of something that belongs to the child. In some cases what is sacrificed is freedom or autonomy. In others, it is hope and optimism. In others, the sacrifice is of the child's feeling he or she has the right to take care of him or herself and not take care of the parent, or not endorse the parent's negativity and have to experience it all the time.

With unhappy emotions in a person that he or she does not know how to deal with (or is not willing or prepared to deal with), having someone else on board can seem helpful. *If I have to be miserable*, the thought can go, *at least I won't be alone in my misery*. The parent might not have as a goal that the child be miserable, but this is the result as the parent puts his or her own goal (remaining miserable) above the child. The child here has to separate from the parent enough to stand up for what he or she knows is healthy. He or she must not give in to the parent's agenda, and assert his or her own in order to live the kind of life that matters to him or her. No one in truth can alleviate another's suffering. Each of us is a powerful, Divine creator who is making a life for ourselves to live in order to learn the lessons our souls have incarnated to learn. Giving in to a parent's agenda centering on some sort of identity as miserable cannot possibly help that parent.

When sacrifices of something about or belonging to the child by the parent creates resentment in the child and/or shame and guilt in the parent, there is work to be done. Each must take responsibility for his or her own experience in the situation as a module in the learning journey of soul while human. Each needs to recognize that all he or she experiences has brought the needed human education the soul set out to create for itself while living a human life. If each of them can do this, and then accept the teacher in this dynamic that the other is, then they can move in a different direction with their relationship. They can then be adults together, and there is room to respect the learning journey—including the blind spots and foibles—of each. This sets the stage for a way of relating together that is more open to and based in compassion, and all parents and children need this.

For Iphigenia's Part

As we receive this story, the innocent maiden Iphigenia is a pawn in great war-related machinations of her time. Agamemnon as a leader appears in this story as somewhat of a disaster. He summons her with a lie about marrying some hero and she shows up as any dutiful daughter would. When she gets there and the set up to kill her is revealed, we hear not one word that she in any way protests or tries to escape.

But don't you want her to? Don't you want her to stomp her foot with her hands on her hips and demand an explanation for this absurdity, this nonsense? I do. I want her to get everyone involved clear on the fact that she is not going to be a sacrificial pawn to right a wrong her father committed. I want her to demand that her father be the one paying the dear price in whatever way works for everyone, but directly—himself. Then I want her to look at the confused faces of the powerless-feeling humans present, all trying to figure out what she thinks she is doing, and demand to speak to the person in charge.[17]

As we live this story we have the choice to submit to the will of the parent. Yet we also can choose to leave behind the attitudes or energies handed to us that we are expected to embody or live according to. We might not always believe we do have a choice, and at certain times in our lives we might not be prepared to stand up for ourselves, but in time we will be. We must come to know the parts of us strong enough to say "no thanks" to the will of the parent and express our own.

Of course, this is not always easy. A parent's plan for us, or grief and misery, might feel overwhelming. From the perspective of a child the parent is big, *bigger than*. A parent seems to a very young child everything: God, Goddess, Source, Creator. That carries power and it is incumbent upon us as we age and grow to find our own power, to release our parents from the appearance and responsibility of

---

[17] I believe Diana would respect such a display and the feeling behind it. The goddess of the hunt is, after all, a notoriously autonomous woman who belongs to no man, cares for herself, and relies on no one for anything. Diana would never allow someone else to take responsibility for what she had done wrong and would never submit to being sacrificed to right someone else's misstep or misdeed.

being bigger than us and become willing to inhabit our own natural selves in ways that are just as big.

That process could be thought of as part of the archetypal process of Iphigenia, in fact. The story tells us that she is a pawn in the greater machinations going on around her. But as we live this story in our own lives, not all of us submit to the situation, instruction, assumption about us, or energetic edict at hand. There are many of us who rise up and begin to stand on our own two feet during these times. *I don't want to dress as you wish. I don't want to go to your alma mater. I don't want to work in the same profession as you or the one you choose for me. I don't want to live where you think I should. I don't want to marry the kind of person you choose. I don't want to live the life you would have me live.* When we stand up to the will or desires or plans of a parent and assert our independence in this way, we are living an Iphigenia story. As this story is a tool for teaching us to submit to the wills of our parents, it doesn't include that thread, but it's very real nonetheless. This story has been shaped this way so that the patriarchy can survive and prosper because, culture shapers know, the patriarchal project is lost if children do not listen to their parents.

The last corner of this story to explore as it regards Iphigenia's relationship with her father is that

Agamemnon summoned Iphigenia under false pretenses, telling her that it had been arranged for her to marry Achilles. What the parent has in mind for us might not be in our highest good, and it might be presented to us with lies—intentional or not. The vast majority of us have excellent radar for lies, but we will tend to trust others over ourselves, especially when it comes to what our parents tell us if we have given them and their bigness any power over us and have not taken it back as we grew up. *We want and need to be able to trust them.* This carries over from when they were everything, the source of food and love. When it becomes apparent that we cannot do so, it can be a hard enough blow to us that we can become willing to believe them over ourselves. We can feel the wind knocked out of our sails, or our lungs even, feeling momentarily powerless to stand up on our own from the shock of the blow. In this light, Iphigenia's story as we live it challenges us to mature by trusting ourselves deeply, in fact more deeply than we trust our parents and other loved ones.

The End

I don't think I can finish this chapter without including some thoughts on how the story ends and how our life stories following Iphigenia's arc do not have to end in the same way.

At the very last minute, Diana, the goddess whose favored stag was killed by Agamemnon, swoops in and replaces Iphigenia with a deer. The animal is sacrificed instead and Iphigenia is flown off to Tauris and made a priestess in Diana's temple. This is to say that as the knife comes down, it is received instead by the deer, as Diana has substituted it for the young woman just the split second before.

There are a few things to note here. The first is that Diana is after everything compassionate, and perhaps we can read into it that she does not (and maybe never did) expect Iphigenia to pay for her father's mistake. When we meet Diana in the story she is not compassionate, but she is speaking to Agamemnon. Killing her favorite deer is not in my mind what she is angry about, but that she can see the character of Agamemnon and is angered that he is the one who did this. Had Iphigenia killed the stag, I think we can count on the story unfolding very differently! So when we meet Diana she is not compassionate, but we have to consider the human she is talking to and about. I believe she can see coming what Agamemnon is willing to do to right this wrong, and she essentially challenges his character by demanding that he sacrifice his daughter. He proves her right, and Iphigenia is not in the end sacrificed but is put in a place of honor in Diana's temple.

Second and related, there is the possibility that the soothsayer did not reveal the true will of Diana in the first place. The whole story turns on this guy's statements. Perhaps all involved needed to learn the lesson to consider the source and not blindly trust what a middleman has to say about the will of a goddess.

The third is that I wonder if we are to accept becoming a priestess at Diana's temple after this nonsense at Aulis as a good life for Iphigenia, a better one than she would have had being traded as cattle in marriage to benefit her father's political and social ambitions. Whooshing her off to that scenario looks to me like a convenient way to end the story because we don't know what to do with the sacrificial child who didn't actually die, the one who didn't go away after the botched attempt to do him or her in. In our lives, when the attempt fails, it is easy for all involved to get caught up in the identity of the child as someone who was supposed to be sacrificed for the parent, and fail to see the rich life waiting for that child, and all the wonderful things that individual brings to the table of his or her own accord.

It feels as though one of the ideas implicit in this story as a socializing and normalizing cultural teaching tool is that children do exist at least in some way as an extension of the purpose of the parent. In the story, once Iphigenia's purpose regarding payment of the debt to Diana is complete (Diana puts a deer in Iphigenia's stead at the very last second), there is nothing else for Iphigenia to do. She will serve for the rest of her life in the temple of Diana, a life of service and humility in our eyes. Perhaps before the event at Aulis her greatest use on Earth in her context would have been to be married off to an appropriate-to-her-father man for financial, political, or strategic reasons that benefit her father and the entire family. Such a life would definitely serve as an extension of Agamemnon's purpose.

As we live this story, what happens to us once we are not after all sacrificed? What happens after we give back the energy of our parent or say "no thanks" to the way of being they would have us perpetuate for any number of reasons?

What happens is that we live our lives.

This is where a gap between Iphigenia's myth and archetype opens up. It feels to me that she is in the story more or less (for want of a better word) useless to all but Diana after the events at Aulis. If we listen to this story as we have received it, we might believe that the end is that we are either useful to the parent or we are to go off somewhere else and stay out of the way for the rest of our lives. But we go on. We can and do live the lives we want to live, bringing our unique talents to the world and in some way, even if small, changing the world as a result. This archetypal process therefore includes going our own way after we refuse to be sacrificed (or after something that is ours is sacrificed and we choose to take it back), choosing and becoming the kind of person we choose to be no matter what the agenda we had inherited from our parents, no matter what energetic or emotional aegis was waiting for us to sacrifice our autonomy, choice, and free will to.

Don Juan and Dionysus: Lovers of Women

*Note: This chapter employs the terms "man,"
"woman," "men," and "women" in ways that do not
have to be gender specific. My starting place when
considering energy is that there are two forms:
feminine, which is, feels, and experiences, and
masculine, which directs, shapes and controls.
Within each person, an entire range covering both
potentials exists all the time. When we condition
females and males to consider themselves in certain
ways based on cultural expectations related to
gender/genitals, the other potential within them does
not go away.*

*Therefore, while this chapter is written as if it's
about men and women, it is in fact about those who
seduce and those who are seduced. And each of us,
regardless of gender, sexual orientation, and sexual
identity, can find ourselves on either side of this
dynamic.*

Everyone knows who Don Juan is: the legendary
womanizer. He seduces women and, when found out,

fights their suitors or spouses in heroic contests having much to do with bruised honor and flashy sword play. Depending upon whom you ask, he is either a most wonderful or most dastardly figure.

This character persists over time in our collective mind because it has captured the imaginations of both men and women in important ways. To men, he is the archetypal sex machine: A go-getter unapologetic about his intense libido and interest in a variety of women while willing to risk much to satisfy his sexual desires. In a cultural milieu that shapes us to fear giving into our natural desires, his story promises a freedom most men are clear few men can have. To women, he is the archetypal lover: Charming, attentive, and truly loving them for all that they are. Even if he leaves once that love has been consummated, the love he brings and inspires is held to be worth the risk of dealing with an angered suitor or spouse who, we can assume, has likely lost his charm and libido or at least has ceased being attentive by the time Don Juan comes around. Otherwise, obviously, she would not be available to be swept off her feet and romanced by this charming stranger. The promise for women is that love and passion can persist in spite of the realities of the settled and stable married life our culture seems to value above all else.

Don Juan is the archetypal lover-conqueror: He gives men the freedom to express the depth of love and their intense sexuality, while giving women the freedom to enjoy experiencing the depth of love and intense sexuality with a man who truly desires them.

But do we even remember Dionysus? Classicists and drama and philosophy majors have a better chance of remembering this god and all he is and does than the rest of us. He is not talked about much these days and, when mentioned, it is usually in terms that we judge. We have come to remember him as the inspiration for drunkenness and a kind of madness that leads to death and destruction. His influence has been shaped by our control-oriented cultures into that of a negative character.

We tend to know him as the god of wine and festival under whose tutelage and inspiration women reveled in his name and were made mad, doing destructive things they, we are told, later regret. And it's clear that they had every reason to regret them given the level of destruction and unwomanly behavior they were seduced into. Dionysus is his Greek name. His Roman name Bacchus is the source of the word Bacchanalia, the drunken festival at which the female followers of the god would get ramped up in enough of a drunken, ecstatic frenzy to do crazy things. We are told that women in these fits tore people, even their loved ones, from limb to limb as they could not recognize them in that fevered and irrational state.

Over time, Dionysus has received a negative face for three main reasons. One is that when people are under what is assumed to be his influence, they lose their sense of self and are not in a space to be controlled. We are to think that control is the name of our game as humans and that we are to be ever willing to edit out our wild, uncontrollable sides into manageable doll-like poses that become the entirety of our lives so that society can survive. If we are connected with the rhythms of nature and know ourselves as extensions of nature (one of the benefits of knowing Dionysus), we will not be willing to subjugate elements of ourselves in order to be controlled firmly by self and other—we would *flow* more. We would be in our bodies and act from instinct; more fully human in the sense that we would not deny our animal nature.

A second reason for this negative view is that Dionysus offers us a way to bring the sacred into our sexuality, to express our sexuality outside the mandate of property-transmission control that is the main reason for the existence of the brand of patriarchy we have been creating and living through for the last almost 6,000 years.[18] Dionysus leads us into the territory of knowing ourselves as the animals that we are, and this is extremely threatening to the culture shapers and maintainers (including well-meaning parents everywhere). Again, when we know and honor all sides of ourselves, we cannot be controlled in the ways that patriarchy seeks to control us. That system cannot survive if we have a sense of natural sacredness in our sexual expression and relationships. At least, anyway, if we have a sense of sacredness outside the parameters of the male gods we have fashioned for ourselves to beat ourselves up with when we do not please them, which we never even really can.

The third reason is that Dionysus is the archetypal lover of women. The model he offers is one of opening women to the Divine through ecstasy and pleasure, worshipping the Goddess through his loving of women. His interactions with women are above all based in respect, admiration, and love for the feminine in all its forms. Dionysus, after all, is a god, but he is a priest of the Goddess, the divine feminine who is behind all the distinct faces of her that we

---

[18] See the channeled volume *Goddess Past, Present, and Future* and the astrology book *Lilith: Healing the Wild* for complementary angles on this history.

have named and portioned off and tell each other stories about.

Think about that for a minute: *There is a god who is a priest of the Goddess and exists to be a lover of women, serving the Goddess by opening women to their natural sexuality.*

Now take another minute—take your time.

This concept is anathema to the distorted mythological framework of Bacchus that we've inherited and updated into the figure of Don Juan. We are to see in our mythologies that there are gods and goddesses but, even when they show up as married or partnered together, there is always conflict between them. We have been taught that there is ever a battle between the sexes played out among the deities, and that this battle is to tell us who we as humans really are. This is a way to say that we are to believe and have been lead to believe that the goals of men and women do not—and cannot—overlap. This is a clear success of the patriarchal agenda: Inspiring us through fear and all manner of red herrings to split ourselves into identifying as culturally-mandated male or culturally-mandated female, depending upon the genitals with which we happened to have been born.

In its current incarnation, patriarchy seeks to survive by doing all it can to diminish the feminine.[19] Patriarchy at its root is a system of property management. It seeks to ensure that property—and therefore power—is handed down through male lines. In order to do this effectively, sexuality must be controlled, and so we have generated the kind of marriage, mores, and taboos surrounding sex that we have. Control is achieved through shaming what is natural so that people fear being just who they are and interacting with each other in natural, desired ways.

We cannot honor the feminine in humans, energy, nature, or sexuality if we perpetuate this version of patriarchy that is sourced in a misreading of human biology. That misreading states that the differences between men and women are meaningful beyond roles in procreation and extend to quality and depth of character; that men and women must be organized in a firm hierarchy instead of being permitted to naturally complement each other and work together. The biological facts include that a

---

[19] See *Living Myth: Exploring Archetypal Journeys* for explorations of several archetypes of the feminine that have undergone serious facelifts to support this agenda (Lilith, Vesta, and Juno). See *Goddess Past, Present, and Future* for a channeled perspective on this. See *Lilith: Healing the Wild*.

woman can have sexual intercourse with multiple partners in a short period of time, potentially preventing clear and definitive knowledge of who the father of a child is. *Therefore, a woman's sexual partners must be limited if the system is to survive.* Women's sexuality, in other words, has to be controlled in order to ensure that men can bequeath their stuff to children they are absolutely certain are theirs, with the goal of shaping and maintaining certain power dynamics so that the system can be perpetuated.

The god whose role it is to honor women and the feminine could therefore not be allowed to continue under the climate of patriarchy without a radical facelift. Transforming Dionysus into a Bacchus, little more than a sponsor of destructive drunken revelry, madness, and wild orgies, is the only way the new patriarchy could deal with him.

Two Lovers of Women

Both Don Juan and Dionysus are lovers of women. At root, each is responsible for awakening in women (or the seduced) something precious. Each brings alive the wild and free spirit in women, connecting a woman to her own sexual energy, the source of her creative power as a Divine being in human form.

Motivation

I cannot even pretend to imagine that Don Juan might not be related to Dionysus or is not a distillation of this figure appearing much later to illustrate conditioned mores and taboos surrounding sexuality. The myth is that of the seducer of women. The god's original part in that had a specific purpose: To awaken women to the Divine through ecstatic pleasure. The later figure's expression of it is devoid of that purpose, as in Don Juan this high and holy purpose has been replaced with what amounts to a hyperinflated libido coupled with the license to give into uncontrollable lust, consequences be damned.

The major difference between these two mythological figures is their motivation. Dionysus at his highest wants to open women to their own divinity. Don Juan at his highest wants to open women to him for his (and, often, their mutual) pleasure. Yet each can approach women with low motivations, too, and this is extremely important to explore as we think about how we live their stories.

Dionysus has been turned by those telling the myth into a low figure, a man bent on ruining the sanity, propriety, and prospects of respectable women by getting them drunk and inspiring them to do insane and inappropriate things. When we live a low sort of Dionysus story, we recklessly seek to open women to and through sexuality. Sometimes we get them drunk or drug them, sometimes we convince them somehow that we bring the secrets of ecstasy. What we are in fact bringing is a personal desire to get off, and now, and then again, also now, and then also some more. Sometimes we convince them that we love them in order to, as the saying goes, "get into their pants."

Don Juan has also been turned by those telling the myth into a low figure, a man bent on ruining fidelity and commitment of well-meaning people who happen to be the glue holding society together. Essentially, he ruins marriage by turning all sexual desire into lust, which is considered negative when it comes to keeping marriages between the right sorts of people together so that society can hold itself together. We live a low sort of Don Juan story when we seduce without love, when we seek to get off by using our charm on women to "get into their pants."

Notice that the low manifestations have in common the desire to get off? When this is the primary goal, connection between humans that opens either to something meaningful and that can create a lasting sense of meaning is not established and, therefore, no one is opened to their divinity. There may be pleasure that comes at the expense of integrity, and there may be no authentic connection on multiple levels beyond genital.

I want to spend some time looking into and behind this. As we have been trained to live together and love, there are aspects of ourselves that have in some ways been trained out of us—if we have let it happen, that is. Not everyone reading this book will identify with what I see as the pitfalls in adopting the myths here as their own, but many will see in their histories and inclinations over time certain tendencies to behave (or act out) in the ways that the myths seem to tell us we must. When it comes to these two figures and their differing approaches to sexuality, it is important to recognize that natural sexuality has been in the collective mind distorted because certain forms of sexual expression have not been openly welcome for quite a long time.

On the main, we are disconnected from natural feminine energy except to see it as something to be used for the benefit of masculine energy, or to see it as the enemy in so far as its manifestations that cannot be controlled. The cultural mind has come to openly hold sex for procreation so that we can fill the world with good little Adams and Eves, and then maybe secretly, in stolen moments or on our own time, for getting off. There is, of course, bleed-through with this, as we do alter how we interact

129

with each other sexually while growing out of and moving beyond patriarchal conditioning. The last few decades have seen what is considered an explosion of sexual freedom, much of it having to do with women raising their hands in the collective dialogue and deciding not to be overlooked any longer. At the same time, cultural shifts have also created a space within which the distortions of natural sexuality revealing the cultural mind's idea that sex is about getting off have become undeniable. The last four decades on Earth have made this before-then meme blazingly obvious, as we can see if we look with any objectivity at the prevailing ethos informing the pornography that is occupying the eyes, minds, and hands of so many people now, even to the point of addiction.[20]

---

[20] I believe that as all humans receive the calls now to process whatever in their souls' various lives has been left undone or not healed, these issues with distorted sexuality that have resulted from patriarchal conditioning over the course of six millennia will continue to come to the surface in loud ways. As it is, individuals are dealing with whatever in their natural sexuality has been shamed over the millennia (the results of which they now carry in their energy fields in the form of painful karma and memories of abuse, suppression, oppression, and distorted sexuality). I feel strongly that as this continues to happen, we will see more and more people realizing that they have at some point along the way turned to pornography to try to fill a need to connect with each other, with the Goddess and the natural feminine, and embrace their sexuality without shame. Though

Before we proceed, here are some notes on when each figure as we live the inherited stories goes wrong.

- Don Juan goes wrong when he seduces without love, and without attention to the effect he is having on the women he is with. He can make of his heart a shriveled black pit of a thing by focusing on getting into a woman's pants so he can get off, by being oriented toward conquest and the stereotypical notches on the bed post, failing to connect in a meaningful way.

- Dionysus goes wrong when he seduces without love and clear intention, but also when he elevates the feminine above his role as the masculine who exists to open the feminine. Dionysus gone wrong includes being soft and compliant when it comes to the feminine, failing to give direction and shape to the experience of the feminine as it opens—failing to learn to hold space for this connection and opening, and failing to be consistent in it.

---

of course few people who turn to pornography for these reasons (even if unconscious of why they are doing it) could admit to feeling better off than they were without it.

As we will see below, each figure offers us a way out of this conditioning, this worldwide, collective epidemic of seeing sex as getting off without deeply connecting to each other, fearing that that's all it's about and for while pining from our depths for meaningful connection.

What We Get

The appeal of living the stories of these archetypal figures deserves some attention.

For the Masculine: Sexual Freedom Through Seduction and Ravishment

These stories hold sway for those whose are masculine when it comes to sexuality because the controls over sexuality introduced as part of the scheme of patriarchy can leave men feeling that their desires are, at least in part, unacceptable. When a man is triggered to desire, there are in most corners of society rules and regulations, at least implicit moral rules and regulations, about how this should be dealt with.[21] But the reality is that when desire takes over, there is no adhering to rules. Part of the nature of the masculine in sex is to want to be swept away in the

---

[21] Pornography is a corner of culture which is the male mind's fantasy world – without rules and regulations – full of seduction and ravishment scenarios.

132

moment of uncontrollable desire for what or who is desired.

Part of the natural masculine as it runs through humans who openly run masculine energy (whether with male or female genitalia, regardless of sexual orientation) is the desire to open the feminine. The urge to control and direct energy comes into play in sexual expression through the male energy by seeking to open the feminine. It is to have the effect of opening the other to pleasure, divinity, joy, happiness, etc. Don Juan and Dionysus in the collective mind have the ability to do this, to have this opening effect on women. Those running masculine energy sexually will feel a need to have an effect on those running feminine energy, and these two mythological figures embody the possibility of having a significant, life-changing effect on those who are feminine.

For the Feminine: Sexual Freedom Through Being Seduced and Ravished

These stories hold sway for those who are running feminine energy when it comes to sexuality because those who are running it need to open and, sometimes, be opened. They need another to focus on them with the intention of transforming their consciousness into the Divine, taking them out of themselves and their normal experience and creating something sacred with them—opening them to being vessels of sacred sexuality. This is not to say that a woman needs or is waiting for a man—far from it. But those who run feminine energy sexually need to be met where they are and then taken into themselves in deep and sacred ways in order to experience themselves fully as the sexual beings that they are. Don Juan comes into town as a carrier of a beautiful and passionate love, and he is looking for the right woman (but women!) to open to shared pleasure. Dionysus holds space for each woman to come to know her own self as the Goddess, providing passionate and attentive focus to open a woman to her inborn divinity through her experience of herself as a sexual being.

Part of the story for those who run feminine energy sexually is that they need to be affected by another, by others. They desire to be met with love as they are and then be transformed into the Goddess herself through sexual love and communion. Don Juan and Dionysus in the collective mind are waiting to do just this for each and every woman with whom they come into contact.

Wherever one falls on the masculine-feminine when it comes to sexual energy, it comes down to feeling that we can open to be exactly who we naturally are. We have been living for so long under the flag of normalizing and rule-dictating patriarchy that the notion of this kind of freedom holds incredible power over many of us, at least those of us who have not given up on the dream of feeling free to be sexual in ways that work best for us and with whomever it works best for us. We feel stifled by the rules and regulations, and we can fear transgressing them because of the varieties of legal charges that can come upon us for acting out our sexual natures in free and open ways, ranging from sexual harassment in the workplace to outright rape in any context, to prostitution and so many other things.

Getting Dionysus Back Into Don Juan

Any of us who has lived the story of Don Juan as it has been shaped in the collective awareness and handed to us has learned that there is, in truth, little to no real satisfaction from series of sexual conquests. Unless, that is, he or she has somehow managed to bury his or her heart deep away from the light of day and the possibility of being affected by others and his or her relationships with them. If we live stories of sexual conquest, we are bound to feel empty inside at some point, in at least some way. The nature of us as sexual beings has us wired to seek meaningful connection with others, to reveal ourselves in the most intimate ways with and to others.

Putting Dionysus back into Don Juan means to be willing to add to the desire to seduce and ravish a conscious awareness of emotion and feeling, both of self and other. Seduction and ravishment undertaken in conscious ways with the intention to love and open another to his or her divinity is a gift, and it brings us fully into our human selves. Don Juan within us needs to be free to desire strongly and to act upon it, yet to be healthy by bringing Dionysus back into the picture, there needs to be time and attention spent working with the energetic and emotional realities of sexual expression, turning sexual intercourse into the path to the Divine that it can be, beyond a solipsistic self-pleasure through an orgasmic conquest of a likely faceless and nameless other.[22]

---

[22] Additionally, bringing conscious approaches to sexuality in general that do not require the destination of sexual intercourse, but explore the full-body, full-heart, full-mind nature of sexuality as it naturally exists within us as humans. My satirical erotica book of vignettes, titled *Modern Love: Fast, Hard, Long, Deep*, includes in many vignettes a focus on what I call "the disposition of the cum," a commentary on pornography's dominant ethos that orgasm *should* be the desired end of sexual engagement.

Dionysus is a lover of women, yes, but he is a priest of the Goddess. Don Juan within us can learn to focus on the nature of the feminine and masculine as embodied by self and other and consciously work to find the right sort of rhythm in seduction that works for each person involved. Sensuality and sex are communication, and Don Juan can honor a woman he is with by paying attention to her energy field and listening to her body, opening her by opening *with* her in the right ways and according to a shared rhythm, not prying her open for his own pleasure.

Getting Don Juan Back Into Dionysus

Expecting to find it only the other way? The sense of freedom, adventure, and liveliness that Don Juan brings needs to get injected back into the polite and socially sterilized version of Dionysus that has survived. You know this guy: He is sensitive and compassionate. He doesn't offend anyone, especially when it comes to women and sex. He is attentive with his sexual partners, always listening to what they need and want, but probably too afraid to take the lead as his natural masculinity would want to do, and probably believes that talking about his desires and needs is, by its very nature, aggressive and potentially offensive and destructive.

For what we could call the new age male, or human carrying masculine energy when it comes to sexuality, soft and sensitive needs to be there, but it needs to be tempered with a clear, direct, passionate expression of desire. Don Juan within us can teach the gone-wrong Dionysus that it is a beautiful thing to bring desire to another, to want to seduce and ravage the beloved. If the Dionysus within is afraid of hurting the beloved, and tempers the intensity of desire, Don Juan will teach that loving another without fire and heat and risk is not actually loving another, but is playing at it, or trying to find a way to guarantee safety that actually throws water on the fire. Don Juan can teach any overly cautious and anemic Dionysus that he will not possibly hurt the other if he's true to himself while being true to the nature of the other with whom he is engaging.

Prometheus: Knowledge is Power and the Gift of Innovation

The name of this figure seems all over our world. He is very well known, but I'm not sure many of us have spent much time looking into his story. The aspect I'll focus on here is his theft of fire from Zeus in order to give it to humans.

The acquisition of fire by humans is widely understood to have changed everything in our collective evolution. It's also true that fire is a potent symbol for creativity and inspiration. We all know that Prometheus is the one who stole the fire and gave it to humans, and we all know that it was a big deal. As I looked into this story when planning this volume, I was surprised at how much came through to work with.

The story begins when Prometheus, a clever demigod known as a champion of humanity, tricks Zeus with a choice between two kinds of sacrificial offering: a yummy-looking thing that is actually filled with gross stuff, and a gross-looking thing that is actually filled with yummy stuff. Zeus picks the yummy-looking one and feels duped, getting mad at Prometheus. Knowing that Prometheus is a friend of humanity and that he takes what happens to us to heart, Zeus decides to punish him by withholding fire from humanity. Prometheus then steals fire and gives it to humans, making Zeus even more angry.

The punishment for Prometheus is to be chained to a boulder and have his liver eaten out by a giant vulture, with his liver growing back daily so the vulture can eat it again the next day. This business is to continue for the rest of time. My trusty *Bulfinch's Mythology* states that Prometheus could have ended this at any time by divulging the secret he had to "the stability of Jove's throne." He would rather keep his secret and go through this daily tortuous horror than give up the power he has over Zeus, the king of the gods.

Living the Story

On its face, this is a story about power and what can become trade in power. It is about when knowledge and skill become currency in transactions that have to do with what makes and breaks power. We live this story when we come into contact with the powers that be (scale unimportant) and bring or seem to bring with us knowledge or skill that could upset their sense or the reality of their power.

140

What Prometheus figures bring is innovation, the gift of change. He empowers the little guy, knowing that doing so decreases the power differential between the those at the top and the bottom of the power hierarchy. Yet when we live this story there is inherent risk as we challenge, stir up, and anger people who are in charge of maintaining the (probably boring-by-now and allergic-to-innovation) status quo. When we take even a little bit of power from those in charge in a given context, they can respond as though their survival is in question, making things very dramatic and sometimes, given the context, dangerous for us.

Each individual's mental faculties combine with experience and inspiration or necessity (or both) to create a unique perspective on the world, as well as unique abilities to view and understand problems. Said another way, each person is a unique blending of a variety of kinds of intelligence, and each of us can bring or come up with solutions at various times and in various contexts. As we do not all share the same kinds of intelligence in precisely the same ratios, we might seem to each other to be on different levels of a hierarchy of smarts. Much about class in the modern world seems to rest upon individuals being deemed smartest, smarter, smart, and not smart, or most educated, etc., which can seem (obviously erroneously) tied to intelligence.

The truth is that we each have an individual genius. Each of us has some portion of fire to hand out to others, inspiration that can change things and make life better. Most of us, however, don't think of ourselves this way, and many who get it do little about it. It is so easy to sit on our individual genius and fire because the risks of challenging the status quo can be (and seem) great. There is also the issue of doubting that our big ideas are, in fact, worth doing something about. When we live Prometheus stories, we are sometimes not entirely convinced that our fresh perspective is really different, or actually worth investing in.

Among those who do something about it, it can be rare that our innovation gets into the hands of large numbers of people, which is usually the ultimate goal of our innovative ideas—to make life better for others in some way. Few of us dream up new things simply to feel clever. We seek to improve processes, quality of life, access to information, freedom, and opportunities for others. We want to see the world become a better, more efficient, kinder, more just, and/or more loving place.

When you have an original idea or innovation to offer, what do you think and feel about it? What do you do about it?

If you hesitate or shelve your idea, you may be opting out of playing a game based in power. There are different reasons to make this choice. When they come from fear, you leak energy, which is your own power. If the choice to shelve it is not about fear, it might be that you are not ready to take an evolutionary leap by offering others your insights. It could also be that you perceive others are not ready, that you must do something else to prepare them for it.

Living a Prometheus story is an invitation to explore our relationship with our own inspiration, cleverness, and our willingness to trust instinct and innate vision. It is a also challenge to get clear on what we are willing to do to make leaps forward and share with others so they might leap forward as well. As stated above, we each possess a native streak of genius—every single one of us. This streak within is linked to instinct. Otherwise it would not be solid in its idea-generating capacity; sure that what it dreams up or envisions is worth the time and trouble to take steps to bring it into reality. When we do access that personal genius, it is personal. It is likely that no one we know (if anyone) has seen clearly what we suddenly see clearly. It is part of this story to envision with clarity something no one else sees or has ever seen.

Therefore, there is a faith necessary to locate and cultivate within in order to live a healthy Prometheus story. When we present new ideas to those who seem stronger or more powerful than we are, we have to believe in the vision of what we are offering. We have to hold faith in the usefulness and worth of what we have envisioned. The efficacy of any inventiveness, in fact, may at times seem to rest on the inventor's level of commitment to it. There are times in this process when we have to evaluate whether the vision is in fact useful, yet we absolutely must be open to this as a check on imagination run amok. Checking this keeps us balanced, instead of viewing each and every time we are inspired to evaluate the vision as an opportunity to be critical of ourselves.

It seems to me that a key to living healthy Prometheus stories hinges on our willingness to let our inner voice of doubt, a natural part of us, to function as such a check. We are all trained to be critical of ourselves so that we police ourselves into keeping in line with patriarchal agendas. Prometheus can teach us to see beyond the constructs that make up social (consensus) reality, into the truth of how things are and why they are that way. This leads to being able to see at times in novel, unique ways how to change things. Living this story in healthy and productive ways that honor this archetype within us requires giving back the fear that comes from our social conditioning about what is worth offering and doing, and how important innovation and genius are. We are trained not to consider challenging those who have been appointed to tell us what to do, yet we each have the inner genius of Prometheus within us. We need to turn the voice of criticism from a harsh judge into one of a concerned elder, one who instead of asking questions about what you are not doing right, asks questions about how you can think and work through something with more intentionality, planning, care, and hard work.

Another note to living healthy Prometheus stories is that this path is for a long while a solitary one. When the gift is ready to be given, we can take it to others. But there is invariably an incubation period once inspiration has begun a process. It does not have to be a long one (because we are after all speaking of flashes of genius), but it is not always immediate. I imagine Prometheus over time observing the comportment of the gods, the attitude of blinded superiority toward mortals. I see him as knowing how things really worked long before he was inspired to steal fire and give it to humankind. He might even have intended for a long while to change how things worked, to turn the prevailing power dynamic on its ear. And when the moment of inspiration struck, he realized immediately that fire was a key to shifting the balance of power permanently. It might be easy for us to see Prometheus as acting quickly, as in a rush to change the world. I prefer to think of him standing up within his moment of genius, fully and firmly feeling the gravity of what he is about to do, ready to risk changing the world forever.

Prometheus stories that are not healthy, for the record, involve rebellion for the sake of rebellion. Disrupting the status quo to make those in power sweat is part of it. Feeling or seeming able to have an effect of some kind, any kind, on the world around one is another. Because living Prometheus stories revolves around questions of what traits and behaviors deserve to be held in high esteem, it is possible to live this story from a place of disempowerment. The thinking would go that if one cannot feel strong and be respected for what and how one naturally is, at least one can make those who do feel strong and are respected hurt, make them squirm, or reveal to others their inadequacies, failures, vulnerabilities, and foibles. This kind of

Prometheus story not only gets us into trouble with those we expose and humiliate, but it invests whatever we are up to with the energy of anger, fear, and pain. Living this side of Prometheus is, at best, only fulfilling in that we have the appearance of being a tool for the discomfort of those in power.

When Knowledge is Power

Knowledge can become power when those in power do not feel threatened by it. It is also when they can see how to profit or become stronger from its dissemination and wide-spread implementation. Good ideas from the creative human mind abound. There is no shortage of life-improving notions and inventions out there.

In truth, it happens all the time that great ideas are seized and launched publicly by those in power in different arenas. Those who run things with smarts know that they must rely on others, including clever people with creative, new ideas, to help them succeed. Not all of them are focused on making a better world (it depends upon what kind of Zeus story they happen to be living!), but there are instances we can see readily in our current globally-oriented context to evidence this.

But when knowledge is power is not really the thrust of this treatment of Prometheus' story, is it?

When Knowledge is Not Power

Knowledge does not become power when those in power feel threatened by it and act to stop it in its tracks. There are of course examples of when those in power catch on to some great new thing that could or will change everything, but in our psyches and energy fields from our many human lives lived on Earth, there is the residue of our training to take what we can get and make sure we don't challenge those in power in any way (if we want to live, that is). There is a rich human history of people bringing truth to power and being harmed as a result.

We also must consider scales of power and areas of influence. A great idea from an individual can be blocked by a particular group, but if co-opted or licensed by an institution or government, it might be more acceptable and deemed more important. The resources and connections of the institution might enable those within it to see how to capitalize on the great idea. The point is that context matters, and we have to consider the source when it comes to others' responses to our Promethean genius.

Wait—Just What is Power, Anyway?

Thus far in this chapter, I've been treating power as if it has to do with influence, money, status, and control. As Zeus is defined as powerful in his role as the king of the gods by what he does and can do, in failing to prevent or stop Prometheus from obtaining fire and giving it to humanity, his ability to define himself as powerful changes. Sure, he can arrange for an interesting punishment for Prometheus that will make others wary of stealing anything from him ever again, but Prometheus has changed everything by initiating a new evolutionary phase for humanity by providing fire. Things cannot remain the same, and each figure's notion of power has changed permanently.

A core invitation of this archetypal exploration is to evaluate what power is and what it is not. Power looked to be one thing before Prometheus stole fire from Zeus and delivered it to humanity, and then power looks to be something else after. Yet each of these two figures lives within different paradigms of what power is and isn't: Zeus's is about controlling the status quo and being in charge, while Prometheus's is about capitalizing on the inspiration to implement a new idea and bring innovation in order to change the world.[23]

---

[23] The reader familiar with astrology will recognize immediately the ongoing, never-ending dialogue between the energies of Saturn (authority, status quo) and Uranus (rebellion, innovation).

When we live this story, we have to evaluate what we believe power is, what we've believed it to be thus far, and what we're willing to let it be going forward. If we choose to allow the status quo to run our lives, then we give into the idea that control is an acceptable definition and model of power. If we choose instead to bring in something new and innovate, then we take power for ourselves.

Living a Prometheus story, you have the option of redefining what ideas and constructs you invest with power. And in so doing, as it happens, you exercise power. You strengthen the part of you that is inherently powerful because it can make a choice.

A fundamental mission of every soul living a human life on Earth is to make choices, deal with the consequences, and learn from all of it in order to make better choices later. The soul-level intention is that the human will learn over time that making choices based in fear, doubt, and desperation do not create power, and that shifting one's motivation for making choices to faith and love does create power. The strength of a soul is its unwavering, unconditional love for all other souls, and we as humans are meant to learn to embrace more loving vibrations over time after cycling through non-loving motivations and seeing what they earn us. We are intended by our souls to modify our approach, learning as we go, ultimately seeing the value of making choices based in faith, acceptance, love, and compassion. Those high-vibrating qualities are all the soul knows, and it is clear that love is power. In the context of Prometheus's story as we live it, there's an important teaching in understanding that innovation for the betterment of self, other, and humanity is a profound act of love, one that reflects the love every soul has for all other souls. Promethean innovation is a step toward embodying the wisdom and power of your Divine self.

What You Get When You Innovate

The story can seem to mean to teach that we have to be careful about when and why we innovate and bring new ideas forward. (You like having your organs intact and inside your body, right?) The story seems to tell us to keep our mouths shut or edit ourselves to make sure we don't tick off the people who run things and have access to large, hungry, obedient birds.

There are actually a lot of these stories that have come down to us. As myth is ever a tool for social instruction, it makes complete sense. The culture we live in needs to teach us the right ways to behave and it is not often in the way that we have set up our world that ticking off the people in charge gets us anything but regret. It would do us a disservice if it did not teach us this.

And yet each of us needs to evolve beyond what and who we have been told we are. Everyone will do so at some point in life. When it comes to Prometheus within us, we can take an active role in this evolution by sitting down with ourselves and asking:

1. Given the various contexts in which I find myself, am I willing to challenge those in power to make positive and lasting change that I believe in when I see what can be changed?

2. Does my relationship with power modulate what I am willing to believe in and fight for?

3. Does my fear limit my passion?

4. What does it mean when those in power don't like what I have offered in the past?

5. What projected result/punishment is enough to scare me into not bringing myself and others into the light and into truth as I see it?

What you get when you are willing to innovate is the opportunity to express an amazing and inspirational part of yourself. It can open others to seeing what is right in front of them and begin making decisions about *their* lives that make them more meaningful, that inspire them to bring out their purpose.

What You Give When You Innovate

You give the gift of genius, which ripples out. Inspiration ripples out, too. You throw a rock in the pond of the boring old status quo and you wake others up to their own inspiration. You send waves out from your own inner fire-bringer.

We've all probably heard that whatever gift you have, it is in you so that you can give to others. Prometheus within us is a primary teacher of this truth. He does not steal fire and give it to humans so that he can feel good about himself. He does not do this so that he can sit around later and congratulate himself for being a clever rebel who stuck it to the man. It is not about him, yet he is also not entirely selfless. We can learn from him to honor the ways in which we are unique, to value ourselves for our cleverness and inspiration to innovate. Once we bring it out, we do not need to wait for a ticker tape parade, but we do need to be clear within ourselves that part of being selfless in a Promethean way is to honor completely our unique individual selves, to never forget that it is the genius of the individual that brings such evolutionary leaps as the introduction of fire—gifts that change the world. Bringing our gifts to the world is not primarily about us, but we in the equation do matter a great deal. Self-negation and -doubt create blocks to believing in yourself, and if you're carrying these energies, it's a pretty safe bet you won't give yourself a chance to make the world a better place in only the way you and your unique genius can.

Giving others the product of our inspiration and unique insight is giving the gift of inspiration and unique insight. In the story, Prometheus steals from Zeus what all involved feel is a right of humanity to possess. Fire was withheld by Zeus, remember, as a punishment for its champion Prometheus. In certain approaches to this story it can be easy to think of Prometheus as a thief, and yet to really get the meaning here, we need to open to seeing him as a fighter for justice and for the good of all. Humanity deserves fire—the literal flame and the Divine inspiration that it represents—and for Prometheus, no god with a gigantic ego and a chip on his shoulder can be permitted to prevent us from having it.

Does Prometheus Ever Throw His Hands in the Air?

I am reminded of Ayn Rand's telling of the Prometheus story in her novel *Atlas Shrugged*. In it, the most important leaders of science and technology withdraw from the rest of society to a secret hiding place in the mountains. They intend to wait out the destruction of the world so they can rebuild it in ways that make sense to them. They are clear the end is coming because of the low level of intelligence they perceive to be running the world. They believe that the regular people who run governments and most industry simply cannot be trusted to run the world in ways that allow them or anything of value to survive. The rest of the world is seen to be squandering the gifts of the intellectuals, and so it must be allowed to die so that something better can be built in its place. Rand's vision centers on criticism that most people are stupid and unmotivated and, therefore, worthless. Her version of Prometheus in the novel is an embittered figure refusing to help others past a certain point. Yes, we all need to have boundaries and not let ourselves be taken advantage of, but healthy Promethean paths are invested in inspiring others in the way that one has become inspired.

The themes and plot of *Atlas Shrugged* are revealing of Rand's personal obsession with judging others for not being as smart or driven or clever or clear-headed or intellectual as she is[24] more than a useful model of how we should live Prometheus stories. When we live them, we must rise beyond our personal judgments of those who have not seen and envisioned what we have. *If we judge them, we preclude the possibility that our genius might be received as a gift and be of help and service to others.* In this way—coming from this vibration—we close the door to influencing them for the better, to sharing our vision. When we do this, we are not sharing in order to make the world a better place, but to be received as smart; to have our cleverness validated. And if we judge them, we also preclude the possibility of being affected by *their* personal genius. Judgment is a double-edged handicap when it comes to offering smarts in the service of making the world a better place, which is at root the high expression in living Prometheus stories.

As Rand lived her own version of the Promethean story, we can observe the results of her experiences in and the emotional impacts she took away with her when it came to standing up within her vision and offering it to others. It is always true that when living one of these stories, we encounter many more people

---

[24] This is her entire philosophy, in fact.

who do not get our vision than those who do. But how will we respond? What meaning will we give to the sound of crickets staring back at us from others who don't get it, this truth that is so clear and obvious (to us), the path forward that makes so much sense (to us)? We in fact have the choice about assigning meaning to it, as we do in every area of our lives. We can, as did Rand, decide that when others are not catching on to our vision it means that they are less evolved, less intelligent, less qualified to be in charge of their own lives and everything else in existence. We can also decide that the new idea we've just come up with is in fact a new idea! We can give others the chance to catch on to what is so blazingly obvious to us. We can explain it as best we can in ways that will make sense to them. We can demonstrate, we can live to model it for them— there's a lot we can do if we're willing to invest in making our inspiration something useful to serve as an innovation for others.

We must continue to believe in it while we allow others the opportunity to evolve—to be shocked into opening to see our vision, or to shift slowly over time in order to be changed by their encounter with us. We cannot know what effect our Promethean gift will have in the long run, in the final analysis. Since genius and inspiration tend to spread once someone steps up and offers theirs, we also cannot know what ripples what we offer may generate, and how they might inspire others to finally, really and truly, honor this Divine gift-giver within themselves.

Nessus: Living in Two Worlds

Myth

A Centaur named Nessus has set himself up in business as a ferryman carrying passengers over the river Euenos. He claims to have been given a mandate from the gods to do so, having earned it due to his moral rectitude. When Herakles and his bride Deianeira come by one day and seek to cross the river, Nessus is hired to carry the woman while Herakles chooses to ford the river himself. During the crossing, Nessus is filled with desire and makes a sexual advance on Deianeira (some say he attempts to or does rape her). Hearing his wife's cry for help, Herakles turns, sees the assault, and fires an arrow through Nessus's heart. The arrow is poisoned with the venom of the Hydra, certain to cause death. As he lays dying, Nessus tells Deianeira that she should take some of Nessus's tunic, stained with his blood, to use as a love charm to ensure that she can keep Herakles's affections focused on her—perhaps someday Herkles's affections will stray, he tells her. She takes the tunic and, years later when she gives it to Herakles after she fears his attention had wandered to focus on another woman, Herakles is poisoned and dies.

Now, that's the story we receive. But as always, since myth is a tool for social instruction, I challenge us to look at what we're being taught by this story. When my attention gets put on a myth, I often get the sense that there's more to it than someone is telling me it is about. Blame my Scorpionically curious self, but I need to understand what is happening *behind* what I'm being told—it takes a lot to satisfy my curiosity when it comes to these stories.

My first exposure to an interpretation of Nessus was in the context of rape and molestation running in family systems with alcohol addictions. A friend had run across this and had begun to do some research. I'd been hearing a bit about Nessus from her for more than a year as she has it conjunct her natal Sun and was working to understand what it means in her life. Then one day it seemed like a good day to spend looking at Nessus and, you know, here we are.

Due to our fears about sexual violence, intimate betrayal, and that we might not be safe out in the world, this myth can look to be about rape specifically or violent sexuality generally. This is certainly an element in the story, but it represents something bigger than any particular sexually violent act, betrayal, or advance.

Archetype Elements and Threads

Following are story elements we can work with understand the archetype of Nessus as it exists within each of us and how it plays out in our lives:

1. Ferrying/Carrying others.
2. Lust, desire, and animal urges; Learning the difference between love and desire.
3. Persuasion, manipulation, and misrepresentation.
4. Establishing legacy.
5. Advertising moral rectitude yet remaining fallible.
6. The energetic power in biological materials – knowing and respecting the energies contained within us (also with theme of uncontrolled desire).
7. Fees pre-established but a greater payment desired due to desire, lust, and/or want—the nature of desire taking over or impinging upon the limits prescribed by the mind.

1. Ferrying/Carrying Others

In the story of Nessus, this ferrying business is literal. Nessus is self-employed as a ferryman, bringing people across a river either too wide, deep, or dangerous to ford without a boat. For any who live a Nessus story, this can be literal but it can also have to do with others relying on the person (or vice versa). The myth tells of a business transaction taking place: Nessus is paid a fee for ferrying people across the river. Responsibility is also a theme here when it comes to being contracted to perform a service on the behalf of another.

Our relationships often become breeding grounds for various kinds of transactions involving reliance on each other. We might come together because of affability, affection, familiarity, love, or some combination of these feelings. But what can sometimes hold our relationships together are the transactions that are set up soon after. These include all manner of what we do for each other and what we avoid doing to each other, depending on the particular people involved and the pains, fears, hopes, and wishes they carry. For instance, perhaps you and I have an agreement that I will respect that you have a difficult time dealing with an addiction or escapist behavior you have not yet faced head-on, while you will respect that I am clueless about how to deal with my parents' treatment of me as a kid (and perhaps now). There are lines of mutual respect that connect people in relationship, and we establish lines of mutual cooperation as a result, setting up these dynamics. Being able to rely on one another in relationship either for safe passage somewhere or around some dastardly emotional or psychological hazard can set the stage for a Nessus story to unfold between two people.

There are times when one person relies on another out of all proportion to the transactions that regularly unfold within relationships. One person might consistently expect another to carry him or her in emotional, psychological, spiritual, and material ways. Using someone as a crutch is an example of this and can set up a Nessus story in a relationship. It is true that relationships are wonderful teachers for all humans and that each of us needs them not just for maintaining health on various levels but also for growth—we need each other to evolve. There are times during the normal unfolding of healthy relationships when one person relies on another to carry or guide him or her through or over the turbulent waters life offers, yet sometimes one person or both get stuck in one end of the carrying or ferrying, setting up difficulty. Living a Nessus story with this theme in play asks us to ensure that we are not relying too heavily or too often on others to carry us to safe, solid, stable ground. Living it means that, in time, we need to become ready to ferry *ourselves* over and through difficult and rough periods in our lives, no longer waiting for, expecting, or even demanding others to do it for us.

This archetypal thread also asks us to stay in check when we are ferrying others through life's difficult, wide, or deep waters. We come together because of love, and love often in time gets confused with the support that is felt through doing for each other. We might question how much we really love another if we are willing to let that person risk drowning in turbulent water—we want to protect and shelter our loved ones from danger, after all. This form of loving—an impulse to protect those we love—is part of what makes us human. But as this story becomes more front and center in our minds, I feel we are in need of checking in with how we function in relationship as both ferrier and ferried. Both sides of the overdependence and reliance on carrying can teach us about Nessus themes, and sometimes we are living a Nessus story by being carried while at other times are we carry others.

2. Lust, Desire, and Animal Urges; Learning the Difference Between Love and Desire

Some of the tellings of this story seem to indicate that Nessus thinks he loves Deianeira but, in the short time that he knows her, it might be safe to trust that it is really lust that he experiences. He is feeling a chemical/hormonal surge inspired by how she appears to him and the feel of her proximity to him (he is carrying her), and he acts on that surge.

The fact is that we are animals. We each have sexual urges at times that are inappropriate in terms of whatever social milieu in which we happen to find ourselves. Societies are formed, after all, to keep our animal natures in check. Many of us live Nessus stories that invite us to recognize the truth of animal, primal urges we typically classify as lust and then judge ourselves into amazingly stifling stupors that breed and encourage later distortion when it comes to natural sexual expression. Anything natural that is suppressed long enough will, in time, breed distortion. After this, attempts at natural expression will come out in distorted ways.

Honoring this primal side of ourselves can be challenging if we buy into and swallow the cultural line that we are to be controlled (by self or other) at all times and that we are to allow our minds to control us. All the Centaurs (except Chiron because of his unique parentage[25]) remind us of our animal natures and invite us to make peace with the fact that we are animals. In time we can learn to come into

---

[25] Chiron is not part of the other Centaurs' genetic line. He was born after the rape of a nymph named Deianeira in the form of a horse as she ran from a lustful Kronos, also in the form of a horse in an attempt to overtake her.

balance with these two sides of ourselves, but to get there we have to come out of living in imbalanced ways sourced in cultural teachings dictating that our minds alone are supposed to be running our lives.

The result of thousands of years of suppression of our natural sexual selves – and distancing ourselves progressively from the truth that we are animals first – is distorted expression of sexual energies. The instinctive primacy of biological urges can cloud our understanding and experience of love if we are frustrated sexually and the heart is not available to open when it comes to sexual encounters. Those living Nessus stories revolving around this thread are learning to honor the animal nature we each possess while also managing connecting to others with the mind and heart. After some sorts of sexual experiences in early life—when hormones rage and primal urges are yet not understood, directed, or married with the wishes and instincts of the heart or emotional center—sex can seem for some to come at the expense of the heart and, for some, the other way around as well. Living this sort of Nessus story challenges us to be the animals we are while directing our animal natures to parallel what is happening in our hearts and vice versa.

There is nothing wrong with full-on animal, carnal lust, just as there is nothing wrong with full-on, heart-open love. This Nessus thread challenges us to honor ourselves on all levels even when there are apparent contradictions in want, need, and the relationship or sexual options that are or seem available to us.

Sometimes when we live this thread of the story we are in need of exploring the difference between lust and love. There are times in the lives of many when it becomes necessary to sort through competing and conflicting urges, desires, and needs in order to tap into an inner truth about the best way forward with one's relationship with self and other. What we are open to experiencing can determine the course of our lives, including when it comes to romantic and sexual relationships. Are we willing to act on desire without love? If so, do we do this in hopes that love follows? Or do we engage in love without lust, hoping that lust will eventually unfold? The two worlds of love and desire do not of course have to be mutually exclusive. But that all humans over the course of many lives along the Earth time line must figure out for themselves the right level of investment in and balance between these two sides of life. Those who have both in the same relationship understand the truth that living in two worlds requires at times a balancing act and, at other times, choosing to invest in different sets of priorities. To the external observer living a Nessus story along this thread (one who is in need of learning to live in the world of desire while living in the world of love), it can seem mysterious and perhaps unattainable. We live this thread of the story when we need to become more whole by allowing all sides of ourselves to participate in choosing, investing in, and maintaining relationships.

There are those living this side of a Nessus story who are shut down sexually, not in touch with their animal, primal sides. The history of suppression of natural sexuality on the cultural and societal levels has lead to a great deal of behavior sourced in and stemming from distortion. Some people in need of exploring this Nessus thread will have experienced others treating them to the kind of inappropriate or unwanted advance that Deianeira received from Nessus, and others will have experimented with making advances toward others with it not going well, leading to shame, guilt, and shutting down sexual energy in an effort not to transgress lines in the future and do more harm.

You'll read more about sexual violence and Nessus stories below.

3. Persuasion/Manipulation

We could also view this story in terms of misrepresentation and, to put it bluntly, advertising. This has something in common with thread #5, Advertising Moral Rectitude Yet Remaining Fallible, but deserves its own entry.

Nessus tells Deianeira that she can use his blood-soaked tunic as a love charm should Herakles ever stray from her heart and bed. There is no reason whatsoever to believe that he believes that this is true. He is, no doubt, doing all he can do to avenge his own murder. Nessus in the moment has to know that he has been poisoned—as a warring centaur he is no stranger to battle wounds. As he dies he sets the stage for eventual revenge against Herakles with Deianeira's unwitting help. Perhaps he assumes that the great Herakles would be sure at one point or another to have competition for space in his bed, being a hero famed the world over for his strength, bravery, and awe-inducing deeds. Nessus might assume that Herakles's bride naturally would have insecurities about Herakles's fidelity when he plants the seed in her mind, thereby ensuring that she would take some of his poisoned blood and use it to unwittingly kill her husband at a later date.

Regarding advertising, Nessus is telling Deianeira that what he is offering her will do something that it simply cannot do. He's giving her a sales pitch—his unavoidable demise now for the eventual promise of the demise of Herakles—and Deianeira plays the naïve rube who believes the lie and enables his plan, buying in from hope, which is sourced in fear of the future.

When we live a Nessus story centering on this thread, we misrepresent something to play on someone else's real or assumed weakness, vulnerability, or fear. Whether that person believes the sales pitch or not, we at least can try! This thread also has to do with being recompensed in some way, perhaps other than monetarily, when we feel we have been wronged. It's also about using another to exact revenge as the only payment we may feel is left to us. The motivation for behaving this way is something other than loving and kind, as it is an attempt to gain more in the moment than might be rightfully ours. It seeks to put a cost on the pain, discomfort, humiliation, shame, or disrespect we are feeling in the moment. Living this thread of Nessus's story, we may feel there's no harm in trying to recoup our losses.

Regarding living in two worlds, with this thread we explore life experiences in which there is a reality in front of us or coming down the pike that does not serve us, and we do what we can to convince others to create with us a reality that we prefer, one that serves us better in some way. Again, manipulating others' hopeful natures is a way of capitalizing upon their fears of the future.

On the positive side of this thread we have persuasion, which is not by definition based on deceit as is manipulation. Persuasion involves working to convince someone to come to your side of an issue and, to be clear, this is not always a bad thing. Some people live Nessus stories with this thread and find themselves in need of convincing another or others of the use or value or their position over other positions. When people's minds are changed, change occurs in the world, and change isn't always bad.

4. Establishing Legacy

When Nessus gives Deianeira his blood with the lie about why she should use it on Herakles firmly planted in her mind, he sets up a legacy for himself. Regardless of whether she would use it an hour or decades later, Nessus creates an effect that lasts into the future far beyond his death. In fact, she might never use it. But for as long as she lives she will be aware of the centaur's warning, and his offer of a way out if her fears somehow, someday come true. Either way, Nessus ensures that someone will remember him after his passing and that his unavoidable and immediate death is not his true end.

Those of us living Nessus stories involving this thread try to extend ourselves into the future by involving others in plans, plots, or schemes that will involve remembering us. This could include inheritances and bequests of all kinds, and it is neither good nor bad in itself. What Nessus leaves behind is poisoned blood he has ensured Deianeira will use on her husband and that will result in Herakles's death, but this thread is not about whether this is helpful or hurtful, constructive or destructive. It is simply about the extension of a person in form or memory beyond his or her presence in a given context or literal lifetime.

We all want to be remembered, don't we? It seems a natural human thing. This is why we create, whether the product is literature, art, performance, or tiny people we attempt to train to, more or less, be like us. We need to have a lasting effect, and one that survives our own death means a lot to us. It offers the promise of immortality and, as we all know acutely well, we will each at some point die. We want to have something to show for the life we've lived, and we want to be remembered as having made a difference.

5. Advertising Moral Rectitude Yet Remaining Fallible

If Nessus's reputation or that of any other centaur (save Chiron) were to precede him to the edge of the River Euenos, no one in their right mind would pay Nessus to do anything. The centaurs are known for bringing chaos and trouble wherever they go. They are famous in Greek mythology for ruining parties and bringing or experiencing unexpected, random violence and destruction. The myth does not say if it is true that Nessus has received license from the gods to open business as he has, only that he reports that he has. To be deemed respectable, he would naturally have to draw on some other source of respectability, hitching his wagon to a person or group that could give him credibility after a lifetime of famed, brutish exploits with the other centaurs.

This thread of Nessus's story involves presenting the appearance of infallibility while clearly remaining fallible. The appearance of moral rectitude has become a prerequisite in Western culture for being deemed worthy of receiving any level and sort of public trust. Those in business, politics and other avenues to life within the public sphere (including teachers and clergy) are held to a higher standard than a person in any other scenario. Living in two worlds for people with this Nessus thread means presenting an apparent moral erectness while trying to figure out how to live in ways that honor their animal natures, which they are always learning cannot truly be entirely suppressed. As we have seen with sex abuse scandals in religious institutions and schools, and infidelity scandals with elected politicians, humans cannot edit out their natural sexual selves permanently. We are who we are—animals—and all attempts to control ourselves out of being who we are utterly fail at some point, resulting in distorted expression or some variation on *crazy*. The question is not if we can do it, but how much damage we do to ourselves and others along the way if we try. Again, what is natural that is suppressed will, given enough time, be expressed in a distorted way.

These situations depict the depth of the problem of distortion when it comes to natural sexual expression. Each person involved on either side of one of these scenarios is in some way acting out the collective fear, anger, and/or pain of the distortion of natural sexuality. It is a global problem, but in the middle of which individuals can find themselves for one reason or another. Individuals are responsible for their actions, yes, but we must also understand the context of suppression and distortion in which we find ourselves so that we can understand the true nature and scope of the problem we are playing out. Putting sex abuse and infidelity scandals in appropriate contexts given our primal, animal natures and the fact that suppression breeds distortion is necessary. And it helps us see more about the real problem, the one behind the headlines that exists in the minds, hearts, and bodies of those involved.

6. The Energetic Power of Biological Materials

This is not a phrase you hear every day but it's important to understand. In the story, Nessus's blood-stained shirt is the instrument of Herakles's eventual demise. Some sources say that mixed into it was Nessus's semen as, they say, he was in the process of ejaculating on, in, or near Deianeira when the arrow from Herakles's bow struck him.

Our bodily fluids and tissues carry an energetic signature. There are different levels to this, and one is that biological material is imbued with the energy of the life attached to it. The emotional state of the being is imparted to or imprinted onto or within the physical tissues, though most people are not trained to be aware of energy on this level or to this degree. Humans experience energy emotionally, and the state a being is in when it dies affects how others experience it later. As one example, humane practices for treating animals prior to and during slaughter has become an important topic with people choosing organic or kosher meats because of the intentional ways the humans breeding and raising the animals chose to treat the animals in life and at the moment of death.

As an archetype within us related to our primal, animal, instinctive nature, Nessus is not alone in inviting us to be aware of the energetic impact of our biological products. In the story, blood is and sometimes semen is referenced, each of which carry a measure of the human life force. To talk about blood being powerful might call up images of pre-Enlightenment superstition and the feared kind of witchiness or vampire, werewolf, or voodoo horror movies, but there is truth here. Our minds might also acknowledge the simple fact that semen emitted from a man during orgasm carries the power to cocreate life, but anyone who has had semen—whether one's own or that of another—on or in him or her knows there is an energetic power conveyed through the transmission of that liquid. Nessus asks us to get to know this reality and respect the fact that our tissues and emissions carry energetic power. Given this, it stands to reason that our intentions and choices when it comes to sharing our biological materials with others enhance or diminish that power, and lend it positive or negative quality depending on our intentions and energetic/emotional states. As one example, if you've had a man's semen on or in you when one or both of you weren't emotionally present or open and connected, you know that it is a drastically different experience than when you are.

Beyond blood and semen, consider that Nessus was affected by his attraction to Deianeira. Even if it began as a visual attraction, while carrying her he was likely biochemically/hormonally activated by her. It's easy to assume in hearing the story that he was piqued by what might have been a beautiful physical body, but we can't rule out that he was chemically stimulated, too. His animal self responded to her animal self—how she smelled beyond any physical odor or scent—reflecting the power of the biological materials each of us carry in the physical body.

7. Fees are Pre-established but a Greater Payment is Desired Due to Lust, Desire, and/or Want

Nessus collects payment from Herakles and Deianeira to ferry her across the river Euenos. This is a transaction agreed to by Nessus's conscious self, but his hormones make him want more from the experience than the money that has changed hands. He's hot for her, and the business transaction gets complicated because he is not sure how to honor both sides of himself. The civilized part of him would hold up the agreement, but he is advertising moral rectitude while remaining fallible. The animal part of him cannot in the end be controlled and he takes or attempts to take from Deianeira more than the agree-upon price.

Living this thread of Nessus's story asks us to get in touch with all sides of ourselves when making deals of all kinds with others. Our minds are usually involved in business and other transactions because, for the most part, the majority of us allow mind to run our lives. Minds are wonderful at negotiating and finding ways to make things work. Sometimes we are confronted later with the reality that we want more than we had agreed to take in payment. There is no shame in primal desire and there is no shame in acknowledging it, but the civilized world in which we live requires that we honor the agreements we make and control ourselves, which is to control our impulsive desires and needs.

This element of a Nessus story requires that we learn to value our desires and urges, our animalistic passions and needs, and factor them into all equations. It causes us to need always to keep in mind who we are on multiple levels even when the situation in which we find ourselves seems to be just about the mind. We can't discount our passions and primal selves when we live Nessus stories if we want to end up better off than Nessus himself!

This thread can seem to the person living the story to be about denied acknowledgment of baser instincts and desires, which can be accompanied by frustration and a lack of fulfillment in relationships of all kinds. The person needs to learn to honor his or her true nature at all times even while trying to live in two worlds—rational and natural, mind-centered and body-centered—with others who have also been trained to avoid honoring and trusting primal, animalistic instinct, desires, and needs.

Living in Two Worlds

When it comes to Nessus, there is always tension and apparent dichotomy regarding living in two worlds. It doesn't matter which two worlds we may be considering. It is not always about our animal, primal, sexual selves in tension and conflict with social norms, mores, and laws as we have thus far explored through the story of Nessus. It could be the place a person comes from versus the one he or she chooses later in life. It could instead be what you believe you should want versus what you really want. The bottom line is that if we are living a Nessus story, we are trying to find the right way to live in two worlds. Two distinct realities seem to collide within or in front of us, and we must figure out how to make things work for ourselves with management and intention, and not too much suppression and distortion.

On the face of it, this tension and conflict isn't good. In this position, we are tense and conflicted. But beyond our feelings in any given moment about the life situation that brings out our Nessus thread(s), it's useful to see them in a greater context. One I suggest is the opportunity to explore our own corner of human evolution. If we think that humans are better than animals and decide that we have transcended the meaningfulness of any comparisons against them, we find ourselves missing out on the chance to witness ourselves as part of the greater world around us. Nessus within our psyches asks us to get in touch with our animal nature while recognizing that we are social creatures living together on agreed-upon terms (living with an awareness of acceptable conventions, mores, and laws). The tension we experience in our lives as we try to bridge two worlds reveals more about who we really are as a species, but it also shows much on the individual level of the opportunities we each have to individuate and step into greater and deeper levels of self-awareness and self-trust.

The variety of tensions and conflicts available to us as we live the archetypal threads of Nessus stories are innumerable. In each corner of modern life we may find ourselves wanting something more than we've agreed to receive in payment for a thing or service, feeling sudden rushes of lust and desire at inopportune moments when we need to have boundaries, needing to present an infallible image of ourselves to get something we want or need (or just to make a living). How we explore measuring our existing self-definition against the primacy of what we feel in the moment is the central call of living with this archetype in conscious, healthy, intentional ways.

A Human Nature

Looking at the Nessus myth, we can acknowledge that the centaurs (again, save Chiron) are closer to their animal natures than we are. It can seem easy to dismiss the animalistic urges within us because we've become civilized and we tell ourselves we value that civilization above all else. But the teaching of the story of Nessus is that this distance does damage to and within us, and we in turn damage ourselves and each other as a result. It hurts to edit who we are because of shame and guilt, or fear of what we might do because we fear our biochemical and physical urges.

Keeping ourselves from the animalistic nature within, we might believe we're keeping ourselves and/or others safe. Remember that the Centaurs (minus Chiron) are famed for being out of control. What does it mean about being human if we can also be out of control? But keeping Nessus and our inner animals painfully under wraps or in a cage due to fear of what might happen if we let them out is and will always be a losing struggle. The cautionary tale of Nessus violating Dieaneira is meant to keep us from admitting that we are animals at our roots, but we can shed this societal warning in favor of redefining what a human is and what human nature should look like.

We have language and other smarts we can use to create and shape the world, yes. But if we can define human nature as including chemistry, instinct, sometimes unpredictable emotions, and fiery urges along with reason, language, and higher thought, we won't find ourselves fearing the reality of what we contain within us. To do this, though, requires admitting who we are while committing to responsible management of all sides of ourselves. If we can do this, then we can create a world full of individuals who learn about their unique natures and turn-ons while not harming self and other in exploration and expression of them.

We are all the time confronted with the reality that we live in two worlds. Simply being biological entities in the mind-centered and brain–controlled environment that is our society shows us this on a daily basis. Social cohesion rests upon the willingness of individual humans to behave according to rules and normalizing expectations. We have taboos and mores and a sense of what it means to be ethical that guides our togetherness, not to mention the institutionalized mores that have become laws and are enforced on a regular basis. In short, if we are to live together and make it work we need to live according to shared rules.

The conversation about Nessus must expand at this point to include more about the people he comes from, the Centaurs. To repeat, all but Chiron are known for being less than controllable. Drinking to excess is one featured theme that follows them around in our mythologies. Cavorting, loudness, and brawling follows this excessive drinking and, at times, injuries occur and/or someone dies as a result of them careening out of control. Nessus has set himself up as a respectable ferryman at the edge of the river Euenos after this sort of shared history with his centaur kin, ostensibly leaving this legacy behind.

It is never forgotten in the mythology that they are half-human and half-animal, with the upper part of their bodies being of a man and the lower that of a horse. Centaurs in their resistance to living controlled lives as do humans and others in mythology are in a way excused because they are half animals. In general, stories of the centaurs function mythologically as cautionary tales regarding those who embrace their animal natures. If we were to allow this part of the self to come out on a regular basis, the culture shapers knew, we would choose not to be controlled, making their job harder. Culture shapers have the job of teaching us how to belong so we can learn to keep ourselves safe within the boundaries of the social group.

We usually don't like this side of ourselves until we feel we have to let go and need to blow off steam. And it is then that we often find we don't know how to manage it, the result being losing control.

Fears of Losing Control vs. Intentional Management

There's something wrong with our assumption that everything about us as beings can be understood through the mind. We insist that thinking and talking about who we are and what we experience can take us to true understanding, but thinking and talking alone can't get to the truth of who we are.

The effects of psychology on all aspects of post-modern life are readily apparent. The evidence of our efforts to explain ourselves in such ways is glaringly obvious in how we attempt to address all of our emotional, psychological, and spiritual issues. First, we talk. Then we try to medicate in some way and add more psychological (talking) remedies for what seems out of order. Then we talk more, until we realize that the medication we're on isn't the right one (because the pain doesn't go away) or we're not at the right dosage yet (because we're not as pain-free as we expected to be at this point with all the talking and medicating).

Psychology, allopathic medicine, and related disciplines permeate our lives to the point that it's difficult if not impossible for many to conceive of a human being as an animal that evolved on Earth over time. The celebrated emphasis on our reasoning and linguistic abilities as setting us apart from "lower" life forms has done a number on us. I believe this is because we have a deep need to feel special and that we matter, and so we tie our ability to feel special to external power-over/power-under dynamics, and we put ourselves at the top of all the lists.

In the context of Nessus, these power issues can come when pained after someone you deeply desire romantically or sexually rejects and/or insults you. It also comes through in the opposite way as when one person overpowers another and, feeling strong, internalizes the power-over situation as indicative of his or her worth as a being. It also happens when one person carries or ferries another and one or both resent the self or blame the other for his or her circumstances.

Living with Nessus in a post-modern world includes getting over perceptions of worthlessness if someone doesn't want you, or worthiness if you can force yourself on someone and conquer him or her (whether sexually or in some other dynamic). We're living in a time that features a struggle to learn to take responsibility for not just our choices and behaviors, but also the nature of who we are. To get into this, you need look no further than the numerous debates about white privilege hanging in the air in our post-modern culture: It's not enough to take responsibility for your own stuff right now, but you've got to navigate if you should be taking responsibility for cultural history in place long before you were born. We're all working this out together, and we're each trying to find our way through confusion and new territory when it comes to conceptions of power and responsibility.

Healthy Nessus begins with admitting who and what we are (animals). From there, we need to shed fear and stress that we need to exert total and suppressive control over the animal side of our human nature in favor of learning to intentionally manage all aspects of ourselves including it. The more any of us lives in fear of something, the more reason we have to fear it. Living in constant tension that we might transgress social mores because we're afraid of what we might do to others keeps an unhappy seed of fear, pain, and suppression watered and nurtured over the long term. Getting to know what inside us we might fear, shame, doubt, or hate is a critical path forward when it comes to the apparently antisocial nature of the Nessus thread of consciousness within. We must learn to exercise these parts of ourselves so we know how and how not to use them if we are to cease living in fear that they might exist, pop up, and take our otherwise well-meaning selves over to create havoc and destruction. In this way, Nessus is an archetype within the human psyche that calls for integration, which necessarily begins with demoting the linear, logical mind from its self-appointed position of supreme authority in our lives. Living with Nessus in healthy ways presents the need for humans to learn to accept all parts of self and learn to work with them so we're not living in fear of them taking over and ruining our lives, common fears of the mind when it comes to the notion that there might be something outside its autocratic control.

Living with and Healing Sexual Violence

Reading the story of Nessus, it's easy to see it to be about rape and violence. But it is really about the reality that we have failed to cultivate the taking of responsibility for our desire, animal nature, chemistry, lust and, even, intense emotions.

When sexual violence and molestation are prevalent with this archetype, it is because it presents the opportunity to learn about our animal nature and taking responsibility for our animal/desire/lustful sides. While it's difficult to live through and acknowledge, there are times when we learn what our souls sent us here to learn through abusive situations (i.e., a lack of responsibility is brought to and modeled for us in order that we learn how to see and take responsibility for ourselves, or power-over attitudes are brought to us to push us into learning more about empowerment).[26]

---

[26] In the soul-centered work that I do with clients, we work with two layers of interpretation for all painful issues, including abuse of all kinds. First, we acknowledge what happened, how it made the person feel, how it affected him or her then and may continue to affect him or her now, and what it seemed to mean that it happened. Second, we add in perspectives on why a soul would cocreate that experience as a vehicle for learning during a

We have to be careful not to rest easy that this story is about rape and molestation—again, it is about the human experience of needing to learn to take responsibility for our lust/desire/urges. The message is not to control these aspects of ourselves (stuff them into a box and not let them see the light of day, which would breed suppression that later comes out as distortion). The message instead is to learn to feel these parts of ourselves without judgment and without fear. We must acknowledge the reality of them and learn to direct and channel them so that they can be expressed in healthy ways according to appropriate boundaries—that we live out these parts of ourselves at the right time, in the right place, with the right partner, and for the right reasons.

My feeling is that the abuse passed down through generations in families is associated with Nessus because of ancestral karma and the nature of living together. This type of karma is, essentially, multigenerational homework which all of the souls

---

human life. Healing after abuse calls for many shifts including taking responsibility for the what the soul has laid out for the human life, adding in a view that honors that each soul sets out for its human selves a wide variety of learning experiences, many of them not pleasant, yet all of which teach the soul what it's like to be human, which is what it got itself born to learn. For more on these perspectives on soul, see all my channeled books.

involved in the family system agree to tackle and try to work through while human. This work of the souls in this group is in attempting to reconcile animal nature and desires/urges with moral strictures and social programming, learning to find appropriate expressions of their animal natures and not give into urges that might cross boundaries and sacred lines. The intimacies of living with people in family dynamics can bring out aspects of human animal nature, and so I believe that families happen to be convenient incubators for much of the learning about establishing healthy boundaries between generations and genders that souls embody on Earth to learn. Beyond the conscious intentions of a person, he or she might at times be triggered by the intimacy generated by the trust of an infant or young child, as bathing, clothing, and tucking in are normal parts of the adult-child dynamic when the child is very young.

When alcohol and other substances are involved in sexual violence—whether occurring in families or not—Nessus's signature may be there. We are dealing with a nearly global epidemic of not knowing how to deal with our most intense emotions, including pain, anger, jealously, and resentment—any emotion that can leave us feeling powerless in the face of it. When we feel emotions that call up our deepest shadow selves and aspects of self we're afraid to confront because we don't know if we (goodness) will win, we may drift toward feeling out of control. Using certain kinds of substances including alcohol can leave us feeling uninhibited, and so it is under their influence our Nessus sides may come out more than usual. The hidden, suppressed, horrible part of us that desires to experience sexuality as a power play so that this part of us can feel vital and valid. In some, knowing that one is capable of conquering another being in some way (including but not limited to sexually) can be a validation of one's existence. Remember that the social, cultural, religious, and filial inheritances most living on Earth now are dealing with are those based in suppression of natural, instinctive drives, painting natural, primal sexuality into corners where it twitches and writhes, waiting for some signal that it's okay to "release the hounds" and run amok. The Nessus, animalistic part of a person wants, *needs* to eschew morality-based control strictures and run wild, to see what feels good and what might happen next.

In the final analysis when it comes to Nessus, substances that lessen or eradicate inhibition serve as vehicles for loosening ourselves out of social and moral constriction, as well as convenient excuses to give into an inescapable animal nature. But, it should be noted, these substances distance a person from his or her intentional nature. I offer that willingly exploring one's animal nature without feeling there must be a substance involved so one has permission to do so can lead to a healthy integration of the two sides of self. Relying on substances to let loose will, likely, lead to further suppression and fracturing of self, ultimately creating more suppression from guilt and shame that will result in time in more distortion that plays out negative Nessus stories.

Penelope and Sisyphus: Why Bother?

Each of these two figures represents a different reason for doing. Each does a boring task again and again, and each seems doomed to do it for eternity. One chooses to ongoingly undo the results of her hard work, the other watches his work be undone against his will and with no recourse.

Sisyphus's story has been treated in a wonderful way by the philosopher Albert Camus in his essay, "The Myth of Sisyphus". And this figure's name in the collective consciousness has come to stand for the work that never ends, and as a symbol of the absurd (I'll explain that in detail in the section below on Sisyphus). In terms of myth, a person is living a Sisyphus story if he or she is engaged in some task or work that never ends, is bound to be undone, or that is impossible to actually accomplish—one that, therefore, seems not worth doing.

Penelope, on the other hand, seems not treated nearly as often. If we remember her at all, it's as the wife of Ulysses, the hero it took so many long years to return home after the end of the Trojan War. Since she is the less well known of the two, let's begin with her.

Penelope's Story

As stated above, Penelope is the wife of Ulysses, the King of Ithaca. They are married for less than a year when he leaves to fight in the Trojan War. The war lasts ten years and he is another ten in getting back home. She receives no word from him during these years as he tries desperately to return (his story is told in the classic epic poem *The Odyssey*), and she has no idea if he is even still alive.

But Penelope holds hope that her husband will come home. She is beset by a hundred obnoxious suitors, the noble and wealthy of Ithaca. Each implores her for her hand in marriage, eager to convince her to accept the to-them obvious fact that Ulysses must be dead. She insists on waiting, and they in effect inhabit the palace as they wait for her to wake up to reality. They become aggressive, and Penelope feels pressured to accept one of them as her new husband so that the rest will go away already and there can again be peace and stability in the palace.

She announces to all that she will make a decision once she is finished weaving the funeral robe for Laertes, the deceased father of Ulysses. Each day she works on the robe publicly, and each night she undoes the work done that day privately. She in this way puts off making the decision she does not want to make.

Sisyphus's Story

Sisyphus is a favorite of ours when we feel overwhelmed by circumstance or life and feel we cannot win or, perhaps, just break even. As modern life has sped up and we have become creatures of hectic habit (as we have become less and less grounded and, therefore, less intentional and sane), Sisyphus's name is invoked and felt more and more as a story we live.

Some details of his story vary according to the source, but the essential idea is that Sisyphus angers the gods and as punishment is sentenced to an eternity of rolling a boulder up a hill. When he reaches the top, it rolls back down again, entirely out of his control.

The Absurd, Plus Nihilism

Before we proceed, it's a good idea to get into a thread that I feel ties these two mythological figures together: the absurd. That word is widely used, but its definition as a philosophical concept may not be fully understood by many. It's the foundation of the branch of philosophy known as existentialism, which is concerned with considerations of human existence such as *Why bother living?*, *Is everything meaningless and maybe I should kill myself?*, and *Oh hey, if everything's meaningless, what about murder?* (If this approach to philosophical inquiry is done well, it's not as depressing as it might sound.) Its central question could be boiled down to: *Is life worth living?*

Regarding the absurd, the idea is that it is in the nature of a human to appeal to the outside world (including the natural world, societies, governments, groups, and other people) for a sense of meaning and purpose, to validate the self. It is, however, in the nature of the universe to be indifferent to that inherent human need. The absurd is the surprise, pain, shock, and anger that arises in a human from the collision of his or her innate need for meaning and the total refusal to provide it by the universe and all its constituent parts outside the self. The absurd sparks and inspires disbelief in the midst of pain, leaving an individual to feel all alone in an indifferent world.

This indifference is felt by most as a negative, a negation of the individual's very existence. And so all manner of endeavors to act out and act on or from the pain, anger, despair, depression, grief, and other heavy and apparently inescapable emotions are pursued, each ending in a sad deflation of whatever hope the individual had of trying to find even a lackluster response from the universe to his or her flailing around in and from pain. The result of all this emotional, escapist, and sometimes addictive behavior is nihilism.

Nihilism is the attitude/stance that nothing has any meaning. It's basically the rut where all existentialists ended up for a long while, and where all of their readers ended up if they finished the books/essays and didn't jump off cliffs—until that Camus person came along. He uses the myth of Sisyphus in his famous essay to lay out his addition to this branch of philosophy, namely that in the face of an indifferent universe, you must make a choice to create, and it is creation (and only creation) that can provide you the meaning you so desperately, innately need.

The word "absurd" has the general meaning for us of something like illogical, inappropriate, and opposed to reason. Yet when you are in the moment of feeling an inner emotional and psychological rupture due to the realization that the universe and everything in it doesn't give a crap about you and your needs, it is the weight and power of the frustration and inability to comprehend that can guide your behavior. Otherwise, regarding something that doesn't make sense, you can laugh or scowl, or you can walk away shaking your head and never come back. But your innate sense of needing to find out that there is indeed a purpose to life—*that there is a purpose to* your *life*—causes the stakes to raise rather substantially. Living in this mode over time, the thinking goes, you cannot help but consider suicide.

So, yes, this is all very serious, and it's not something you're ever going to want to think about too much. In fact, you'll tend to do so only when you have no other choice as you attempt to try to figure out how you're going to live in the world given the way being alive makes or can make you feel. But this is where Camus's addition to this garden path comes in handy: When you make a choice that creates, you generate the meaning you can get no other way, and there's an empowerment in this. Then you learn that the feeling of the absurd (and the concomitant wondering if life is worth living or even *can* be lived) will come up again later, highly likely the very next day if not just an hour or few minutes later. Camus instructs us to make the choice to create on a daily basis, to intentionally put our attention and energy in one direction or another, toward one end or another. When you get this, and when you get into a good groove with it, you find that you no longer need wonder about life and its worth because you're in charge: *If you want life to be meaningful, you'll choose to do something that creates meaningfulness with and within your life.*

And it is this level of responsibility for one's life that, in my view, is the vehicle through which we learn about Divine power of choice discussed "Paris and the Power of Choice" earlier in this volume. If you're stuck in *why bother?* for a while, you're not going to be able to see the point in making *any* choice. Imagine a student of existentialism, one without exposure to Camus's remedy for the pain and anguish of the absurd, being offered bribes by three goddesses in the course of a beauty contest for which he is suddenly and inexplicably the sole judge. Imagine the look on the face of that student shaped by repeated confrontations with despair, wondering if life is worth living, carrying heavy and not-to-be-discussed depressive feelings daily, expected to choose between the prizes offered Paris. That entire situation would be meaningless to him, and I imagine him staring at the person speaking with a bit of a furrowed brow from confusion, not sure why what seems to be happening is happening.

In other words, you can't make a choice if you don't care about life, your life, or the world and your place in it. Camus did not identify as an or accept the label "existentialist," but stated that he was taking a stand against the nihilism he saw in the world. This is, in fact, in line with his own portion of creating something meaningful out of the anguish of the absurd. In my view, he may have agreed that the more one gets caught up in labels, the less one is able to be present and engage with what in the world he's ready to meet and respond to.

Reasons For Doing; Your Relationship with a Task

Now that you understand the awfulness of the experience of the absurd and the shininess of its solution, let's get back to Penelope and Sisyphus.

Penelope's relationship with her task is sourced, as stated above, in hope that her husband Ulysses will return. We can view it as faith, whether in him or life, the gods, or justice, or the power of romantic love—no matter. The point is that it keeps her going. But isn't it possible that she's living an Orpheus story of not being able to let go (remember that he and Eurydice were also married only a short while at the time of her death), wallowing in a wish and a hope that Ulysses will come some day? Or, instead, maybe she's rooted firmly in a deep faith that her present circumstances are not the life meant for her; will not or cannot be her destiny. I believe the meaning derived from why she nightly unravels the work done on the robe during the day will be obvious to the reader of the myth, but that the meaning will in each reader's estimation depend upon his or her orientation to faith, hope, justice, the enduring power of romantic love, etc. If you think that love is worth waiting for against all hope, then you'll consider her and her waiting to be noble. If you believe that the universe can't be cruel enough to rob her of her husband, her one blessed love, then you'll see her as a faith-fueled figure with every right to indefinitely overlook the hundred dudes crashing in her palace just waiting for her to wake up to what they trust is reality. Conversely, if you believe that romantic love is hooey and the universe a cruel place devoid of meaning (if you've read the existentialists before Camus and didn't find a cliff to jump off yet), you'll see Penelope as a silly figure denying reality, daily choosing to waste her time and persist willingly in meaninglessness and futility.

From an archetypal perspective, Penelope is keeping busy. We've all done that. She's putting off a choice she seems to have decided she shouldn't have to make. We've all done that, too. She is in a holding pattern, and it's one of her own choosing, of her own design. She's entirely responsible for the situation she's in, and she knows it. The hundred obnoxious suitors occupying her home simply aren't of interest to her, and they aren't acceptable as mates. Her investment in her situation is illogical—appearing ridiculous to the suitors—yet it is her choice and there is a definite logic to it.

Sisyphus, on the other hand, is stuck where he is. He has no choice about rolling the boulder up the hill and then watching it roll back down again. As stated above, Camus uses this story as an illustration both of the absurd and of his unique solution to/through it: Sisyphus can choose to be attentive to this task, *he can choose to participate*. Camus offers that this is the only way he will derive any sense of meaning or purpose from what has become his reality—and will be so for all eternity.

The task is in front of Sisyphus. He need not seek it out, he need not develop any sort of philosophical or moral stance in order to esteem it as worth doing. He pushes the boulder up the hill as he does because he cannot avoid it—he is under the compulsion of the gods. This is where he is and, regarding his life and his prospects, this is it. He has arrived at his final destination.

Archetypally, we experience certain things in our lives as meaningless exercises in putting our energies into what will inevitably turn out to be futile. For Camus, the way through the nihilism that can often result from the inner rupture of the absurd is to choose to be present to what's in front of us. And so the myth of Sisyphus teaches that life is or *can* feel meaningless, a collection of the endless repetition of futile tasks. As we live the archetype, we repeatedly confront just how we will approach the reality that the boulder is in front of us, that the hill is there, and that we have no choice but to push the boulder up the hill. For Camus and for me, it is your relationship with the repetitive task that is everything.

Meaning and the Creative Act

As explored above, the meaning that you need can only be created by you. If you're putting off a choice you need to make or believe you should not have to make, let it be okay. Be in the space of not deciding, and own that as a choice. If you're stuck in a rut and trying to figure out how to feel good—or even merely neutral—about proceeding in that space, let it be okay. Be in that space and own it.

You can't get the meaning you innately crave (and, in fact, need in order to be willing to live) without creating it. And you can't create it without making a choice. And so this all comes down to making choices, which is another way of saying *creating*: Putting your time and energy in one direction or another is a creative act. Choosing where and how to earn and spend money are creative acts. How you respond to other people in your life and how to participate in your community and world are, too. Saying "yes, please" and "no, thank you" to small and large situations in your life also fits the definition.

Essentially, everything you do is a creative act. The trick here to come out of one kind of meaninglessness or another is all about deciding what kinds of actions you will choose.

And, So, Why Bother?

What do you want your life to look like? What kind of effect do you want to have on other people?

What makes you feel good? What makes you smile? At what are you curious to find out that you might be good or, even expert?

What experience would you like to have? What part of yourself would you like to get to know and exercise?

All of this to get here: What game will you choose to play with your life? If we're all born to grow up, mature, age, and die, and along the way we're all guaranteed to encounter numerous shocks from the absurd waking us up to what's really happening around us, it can be easy to view life through the lens of a game. Since you're going to die someday, you can certainly choose to see the time between birth and death as worthless, or not possibly holding promise. But what if you didn't? What if you were to accept that there's also a playful way to view the whole process? What if you chose to live through making choices and watching to see what happens when you do?

What you value—what you consider to be important—can be a starting place for playing this game willingly. Personally, as one example, it matters to me when people can understand their lives and—in some way, to some degree—come out of suffering from being/feeling stuck inside a box defined by unhappiness and/or despair. So, for myself I begin with the question, "What do I want my life to serve?" Then I do what I can to approach it as if it's a game.

Can I teach you something I've channeled, meditated on, experimented with in my life or professional practice that can help you? Yes? *Score!* Can I somehow, in some way and to some degree, inspire you to ease up on the self-judgment stemming from whatever in your life past or present triggers self-judgment? Yes?! Really? *Score again!* Hey, this is a game I can get into. And, to boot, it's fun when I win, and I'm inspired to keep trying to improve my play when I don't win. So, I spend time and energy seeing how good I can become at it and enjoying the effects it has on other people. Said another way, I'm creating the meaning that I need to keep being willing to live through playing a game to see if I can help you ease out of unhappiness, being hard on yourself, and other places humans can sometimes get stuck.

You're a soul living a human experience to try to go from choosing to inhabit and broadcast fear frequencies into choosing love frequencies—this is the mission of every soul while incarnated as a human. It's the love stuff that is the true nature of each soul, and so it's kind of rooting for you to figure this out. In effect, your soul is playing a game here as you, a person living human life through the lens of personal conditioning, thoughts, feelings, and attractions/revulsions. And so I offer you this: If your soul is playing a game as a human, why can't you view life this way, too?

How to Persist, or Some Implications for Those in Existential Crisis

Penelope does what she does to put off what seems to her an inevitable, undesirable conclusion. Sisyphus does what he does because he has no choice. Camus invites us to imagine that Sisyphus embraces his task and chooses to find meaning in doing it because the task is the only thing to be done, and the choice to meet it consciously and with intention is the only way to navigate the situation while making anything out of it. Camus's point is that the experience of performing the task—the presence that comes from engaging willingly with what's in front of us—is the path to creating the meaning we seek and, in fact, desperately need.

My suggestion for how to persist begins with the recognition that there are times in the course of your life when you'll feel that you're futilely pushing a boulder up a hill, and the boulder will roll down again when you're done, living a Sisyphus story. At other times in your life, you'll choose to put off creating meaning, as Penelope undoes at night the work she does during the day. These things *will* happen—you cannot escape these realities of the human condition. These archetypal threads are normal for humans to experience. They are entirely natural portions of the human psyche, and it's best to stop judging that we sometimes have a crisis of meaning, a loss of hope, or a doubt that anything is worth doing.

Recognizing that this is part of the human trip as souls incarnate here to attempt to identify some source of meaning for themselves while human, also be willing to feel the conflict, pain, confusion, and disbelief of the absurd. Choose to take the collision of your need for meaning and the apparent indifference of the universe surrounding you as a cue to let things in your world and self-definition be shaken up. Don't step away from the surprise of the absurd and then retreat to business as usual, hiding and denying what you saw about yourself and the world under a thick mantle of modern, stultifying, boredom-inducing life—this is when depressiveness and despair can take over. Be willing to feel the pain of the collision and *then choose to do something with that surprise, chaos, and fire.* Take each instance of finding out that something outside you is meaningless or cynicism-inducing as a spark to remind yourself that you and only you can create the sense of purposefulness that you need to feel in order to be willing to live.

A Girl Eating Ice Cream

One of my first coaching clients years ago put my attention on the context of what she'd been experiencing in a particularly intense astrological transit, one from the planet Pluto to a body in her natal chart. She reminded me of the contours of the difficult things she had been experiencing for a few years (these transits take a while to unfold as Pluto moves pretty slowly in the sky) and asked something close to, "But how I can acknowledge that I've been to hell and not ruin things for others around me?"

From one of her spirit guides, I was fed an image: She's in a park on a sunny day, and people are doing the kinds of things people do in parks on sunny days. She sees a little girl holding an ice cream cone, engaged with the taste, the cold, the texture. Maybe she's laughing, maybe she's focused intently on her senses. The guide said that my client could choose to enjoy witnessing the girl experience and enjoy the ice cream cone.

Knowing what she knew about what we call darkness, having descended into the depths of depressiveness and wondered with all seriousness if life is worth living, my client could choose to engage with the reality of the human dance in the world around her. She could accept that humans sometimes can feel as if in hell, and then can re-emerge into the light of day and be with others again, bringing with them what they learned but also bringing a willingness to open to joy again. Implicit in this image and invitation to my client was the guide's recognition that life is not easy, and its intensity and difficulty do not always make sense, but we can choose to participate through engagement with life and the world around us.

This is a teaching for coming out of the nihilism and despair that can accompany Penelope and Sisyphus stories. And, remember, we *will* live them.

The important part is how we choose to view them and incorporate their natural, archetypal human experiences into the greater fabric of our lives and self-definition.

Oedipus: Pain, Karma, and the Fallacy of Destiny

The story of Oedipus is undeniably famous. Sigmund Freud popularized it, and the fear that his take on the psychological side of things might be correct has emblazoned it in our collective awareness. The way it is told seems at the very tip of our tongues—so ingrained is it in our mental programming—but there are a few shortcuts through it that our obsessions with Freud and the possibility that he is in fact right (and all that would and does mean about us) leaves us forgetting some of its dimensions.

Forget all of that for a few minutes. You might go for it or not, you might identify with some part of Freud's interpretation of the Oedipal story and you might not. I want to tell you the story from the ground up and offer what I see about the sacred psychological side of it that has nothing to do with Freud's issues with his parents.

The Story

Laius and Jocasta, king and queen of Thebes, want children. They have been married what seems a long time and they are wondering where their long-desired, beautiful family is. They consult an oracle and are told that if Laius has a son, the son will kill Laius and marry Jocasta. Obviously, this will not do, but Laius as the king must have an heir, so they go at it until Jocasta gets pregnant and gives birth. The baby is a boy and they remember the prophecy. They tie his ankles together so he cannot crawl and give him to a servant to take out onto a mountain to leave there to die.

The servant retains his humanity and cannot do as instructed. He instead takes the infant to a nearby shepherd to raise. Somehow the boy is in time passed to Polybus and Merope, king and queen of Corinth. They are childless and have no horrific prophesies lying around to keep children out of their lives, so they adopt him as their own and raise him.

There comes a day years later when someone tells Oedipus that Polybus is not his real father. Polybus and Merope do not tell him the truth when asked, yet he persists in seeking the truth, eventually going to the oracle at Delphi for the real answer. The identity of his parents is not revealed there, but he is told by the oracle that he is destined to kill his father and marry his mother. This inspires him to leave his home at Corinth in order to ensure that the prophesy cannot come to fruition, assuming that the father and mother in question are Polybus and Merope.

On the road he meets an argumentative old man who happens to be Laius, his birth father, but neither has an inkling that they are related. They fight over who has the right of way and Oedipus kills Laius in self-defense. He continues on to Thebes and, in the process, comes to the Sphinx, asking its riddle of all who try to pass, harassing all who come near Thebes. He is the first ever to answer it correctly, and so the Sphinx kills itself. He goes on to Thebes and is rewarded for freeing the city from the monster by being appointed king, since they just recently lost theirs. He thereby fulfills the prophecy by marrying his mother.

Things seem great. He and Jocasta have four children together. In time, Thebes is afflicted with a plague of infertility that affects both humans and crops. Oedipus sends Jocasta's brother to Delphi to get the scoop on how the plague can end. He learns that the murderer of King Laius must be found and brought to justice. Oedipus pursues this and is told by a seer to stop looking already. But his people and his kingdom are sick, so he persists. They argue as he presses the seer and is told that he himself is the killer. Oedipus sees that he is responsible for the plague, and the truth about his birth in Thebes, and the prophecy comes to light. He takes his own eyes out in shame and spends a great deal of time wandering the countryside, a broken old man with a daughter as his guide, until he dies.

As We Live Oedipus' Story

We live this story when we are told what will happen if we continue on the course we have chosen and we do not deviate from it, feeling it is out of our control.

We also live it when we listen to others about what will happen and then, when it does, assert that we never had control over it in the first place: *It had to happen because it was always going to happen.* The concept of destiny can be used as a crutch to avoid taking responsibility for our actions in a given moment, but giving it credence is, in fact, a reflection of the deep sense of powerlessness we as a collective carry about why our lives on Earth have unfolded the ways that they have. It can also be a convenient scapegoat for whatever in our lives seems that it went wrong.

We inherit from our families all kinds of ideas and attitudes. As an example, some of these might be about what happens to people in our family when we age. There are ages people are taught overtly or otherwise to fear. We learn that what happened regarding health and wellness and, sometimes, even in method of death, to our grandparents, parents, and other ancestors will happen to us. Genetics are real yet our energetic susceptibilities to illness and disease, the chance that our genes will be triggered and the situation will come to pass in us, is not set in stone. Our energy fields are our own energy fields, and whether we are operating them with conscious awareness or not, they are functioning to create our external lives to reflect our inner dynamics.

We live this story when we believe that we do not have free will or choice, that life has to be a certain way. In the myth, Oedipus walking into disaster after being told that he would is meant to instill in us a belief that, even when we have some key piece of data that we could use to change or prevent a scenario, we won't. Alternately, it could be seen to be intended as a warning to the human ego to accept that even if we were to try, it would fail: *There are things beyond your control. There are terrible things that will happen no matter what you do.*

When tragedies do occur, we should ask ourselves if we could have seen it coming. It's natural to do so. But to punish ourselves for not being able to change

215

or avoid something that's outside of our control isn't the right way to end the story, as Oedipus does, wandering defeated through the countryside, knowing he's ruined everything and living out his days as a destructive, unredeemable failure.

One thing we might not know or remember when we edge into the territory of Oedipus stories is that every human has free will, and every one of us is just as powerful a divine creator as all the others. We must give ourselves permission to make mistakes because they are a major factor in how our souls learn about being human. But we also need to give ourselves the benefit of the doubt that, sometimes, we can't prevent tragic circumstances because another being—or other beings—involved are powerfully vibrating their own free will as well as their unconscious fears, doubts, guilts, shames, etc. We are each creating a set of external circumstances around us based in our unconscious vibrations, including what we unconsciously believe to be true, right, and real. No matter what you do or tell me, I might be set on creating my unconscious beliefs. No matter I do or tell you, you might be set on doing the same.

Therefore, it is important as a part of spiritual maturation to respect what we and others are creating, even if it's painful. When we love others, we of course want what's best for them, and the same goes when others love us. The story of Oedipus is one of a string of tragedies that didn't need to happen, and it was a combination of human misunderstanding/assumptions, arrogance, and forgetfulness that seems to be the reason it happened the way it did. But those who live Oedipus stories are learning something important: To either give into the disempowering notion that they have no choice because of destiny (or fate or disempowered views of karma) and live into that disempowerment, or to choose to take responsibility for at least finding out what in their lives *can* be changed.

Here's a hint on the bigger picture in play for all human lives: Every soul sends its human selves to live on Earth to attempt to figure out how to go from making choices based in fear and pain into those based in acceptance and compassion. In other words, it's normal for humans to find themselves in pain and believe that's the only thing for them to live within and from. It is in somehow figuring out they have a soul, and that loving empowerment is its true nature, that the possibility for true power comes into view. Real power in terms of the Oedipus story isn't the ability to prevent disaster. True power here comes from engaging consciously with the world and others around you as bringers of opportunities for you to learn to go from fear, etc., into love, etc.

And so, as we consider the archetypal path of how we live Oedipus stories, I offer you that it is easier to choose to not take responsibility for pain and tragedy, awful things that our human minds and reasonable selves feel they can't explain except as evidence of being worthy of punishment. Said another way, it is preferable to assume someone or something else (God or fate/destiny, respectively) is punishing us over to attempt to open to the truth that there's nothing wrong with the experience of pain while living a human life.

The truth is that we will never be able to eliminate pain, suffering, and hardship. Will we let that mean that we're being punished for doing something wrong or being the wrong kind of person? Will we beat ourselves up because we feel beaten up and feel we need to try to figure out why we deserve it?

A Deeper Look: Destiny, Karma, and Consciousness

The single major thread in this story is that there exists such a thing as destiny. But there is not—it is a fallacy. At each step in our journeys, we each have free will and choice. At each step along our way we can change how things go.

The notion of destiny has been a problem for humans for gazillions of years, or for as long as there have been humans. We seem to need to believe that there is a governing principle at work or, in many minds, a bearded white guy on a marble throne with a grand plan who runs things in our lives and lets us know with vindictive ardor when we are not living up to the standards of that plan. It can be threatening to our emotional health to take away the power from some governing force or marble-throned old white guy and accept responsibility for what happens to us, but doing so is the next step in our evolution as humans. Our path to evolve consciousness now points in one direction: Letting go of our millennia-old conditioning about who is or might be running our lives and reorienting to an awareness of our true natures as energetic beings constantly manifesting what we're vibrating.

We are energetic beings. Our lives unfold as they do because of the energy that we hold in our fields and, therefore, psyches. We have yet to grasp just how efficacious our energy is in creating the world around us, in fashioning our experiences and the circumstances of our lives. Living in dualism supports and promotes the idea that we are not in charge of ourselves because we interpret what comes to us as acting upon us with no regard to our free will. The idea that there is an external creator and regulator of some sort with a master plan runs rampant in the collective mind. It is at best challenging to understand how we would create unhappiness, trauma, disease, loss, and other sources of pain for ourselves, so we manufacture and then appoint some kind of divine figure to the position, saying that we cannot with our measly human minds comprehend its complex, multifaceted will. We thereby construct a box in which to live, choosing to remain at the mercy of that figure's whims and decisions. For much of human history, we've decided it's easier to believe that someone else is doing these things that make us suffer and that the reasons it does so are beyond us. It is easy, in other words, to be and remain powerless.

But this powerlessness is our past. Our present is the task of becoming deeply aware of all the ways that this history has shaped our consciousness and, therefore, the ways that we shape our lives as powerful, Divine creative beings. *When we do this, we will be able to see how to choose to change it.* We will unearth the truth that we have the capacity to choose in many ways and on many levels how our lives unfold, which will put us in touch with deeper levels of our true creative nature as divine beings.

We most certainly can comprehend the (higher, beyond-the-human-mind) reasons these things happen. *But to do so, we have to change our minds about who we are and what life is for.*[27] We have to choose to see life not as a struggle for safety and security against a judging god or universe, but as a playing field for opportunities to learn what our souls have embodied in human form to learn.

Our future is in working with ourselves in modes that begin with an understanding of the true nature of soul and consciousness, what we are really doing here as humans, and what it takes to fulfill its mission to learn about how to be human. If we do not begin with this understanding of our true natures, with the energetic component of us that sets the stage for all we experience, we set off without a strong foundation and, more often than not, set ourselves up for self-judgment for the painful situations we create and walk into as if blind but should have known better. The true spiritual evolution waiting for us at this time is not more light and ascension into fluffy cloud-inspired head spaces, but getting grounded in our true natures as energetic beings creating our realities by holding the energies (and, therefore, emotions and karma, which are beliefs attached to emotions) in our fields.

---

[27] See *The Soul's Journey I: Astrology, Reincarnation, and Karma with a Medium and Channel* for more.

There is no such thing as destiny. What seems like destiny is in actuality the unfolding of seeds of energy that we ourselves plant. These seeds grow when we maintain an investment in the meaning of both our past and present painful experiences. The definition of karma in my tool box is of beliefs wrapped up or entangled with difficult, intense emotions we might not know how to deal with. Karma is developed when we get hurt in some way or another and perceive that we identify an obvious cause that allowed that hurt to happen. We connect the dots in the best way a human mind can: Factor A was in play and it allowed Situation B to develop, and then I was hurt due to Circumstance C. Therefore, when Factor A is in play, it's probably true that pain is coming.

The more we believe something along these lines, the more we get stuck in a groove, as when a record skips. When the thing keeps happening, we invest even more heavily in in our presumed cause-effect scenario as truth. Of course we do, right? It keeps happening, so it must be true that it has to keep happening. And we will always come up with a narrative to explain why it keeps happening. As a result, the belief about the pain and how it comes to be deepens in our field—we strengthen our attachment to it, even if it hurts and we bristle and spasm against it. This is the nature of karma: We only believe such an explanation for pain to be true because we keep seeing it happen in front of us, but the only way it can keep happening in front of us is because we believe it to be true or that it must happen. The catch-22 shape of it makes it seem that no matter what we do, it keeps happening, and this can make it easier for us to attribute it to fate, (a disempowered view of) karma, or destiny.

A major portion of our beliefs are, it must be noted, stored in our unconscious repositories and are sourced in many lifetimes. What happens to humans who are connected to your soul on other parts of the Earth time line (we often call these "past lives," but I refer to them as "your soul's other lives") can bleed through into your unconsciousness in this life as memories you mostly don't realize you have. But they vibrate difficult emotions from under the surface and so contribute to the shape of your life. So, while you choose to vibrate certain ideas, beliefs, and attitudes, those of your other-life selves are also vibrating from the unconscious … and are just as strong.

As we carry these unconscious vibrations, they broadcast energetic signals. The fear, pain, doubt, guilt, shame, or other content they contain sends out a powerful signal that should be considered a divine command. Other people and situations that fit the energetic signature of that signal come to you as if by magic, heeding the call of your divine command. It's a sort of magnetization to you of what you (unconsciously) hate, fear, regret, and so on, and it's persistent enough that it looks fated to you—it looks like it's destiny because it keeps coming to you even when you (consciously) want it to stop. This is why so many of us carry a belief that karma cannot be changed: We think it's clearly a reward-and-punishment deal and, obviously, we're being punished all the time with this stuff we don't want to have to deal with and, clearly, don't deserve. We've come to believe that we get good things now if we did good things in the past and get bad things if we did bad things then, which is a simplistic and childish way of attempting to explain why bad things happen to good people.

Listen up: The real reason they happen is because a human is a soul living an Earth-bound life, working out what it means to be a human, and this includes having all manner of possible experiences, even painful ones. It's that simple, and when we can let go of karma as an apparent indicator of the degree to which we must be deserving of punishment and censure, we'll be able to see how to more intentionally create our lives given our unique paths that include working through some painful things that are just part of the human story.

In my eyes, one reason the reward-and-punishment conception of karma is so easy to give into is that we seem to believe that pain is a marker of having done or been wrong, or maybe of not having done or been good enough. But pain is simply part of the path of all humans—all beings on the planet, truth be told. The assumption that experiencing painful things must mean that we deserve them stems from the perception that we are at the mercy of an external, judging force or entity, as well as that we are inherently flawed. And so, in an important way for me, the meaning of Oedipus's story rests upon how you conceive of why pain happens, why tragedy occurs, and why people hurt themselves and each other. If you believe it's because they deserve it, you might get stuck in a disempowered conception of karma. We can expect the same or similar if you believe it's because awful things are inevitable or any other disempowered belief about the origins of pain. However you decide to treat the meaning of this story, your buttons about fate, destiny, and justice are bound to be pushed.

We-as-Oedipus must accept responsibility for our choices, yes. We also need to attempt to reconcile the human conditioned tendency to judge the self for having caused pain to self and other with the higher truth that we are all works in progress, learning as we go through making choices and dealing with the consequences.

And so, as with everything else, you can live into Oedipus stories that end with the tragedy of blame and self-hatred, figuratively tearing out your own eyes for having messed everything up at every turn. Or, you can decide to see all that comes to you as an invitation to learn more about the unconscious issues that you carry that you must resolve and release in order to grow.

As your soul watches you navigate the complexities of human life, it is acutely aware that you feel separate from the source of love, or the Source, or God/Goddess consciousness. It knows that you don't at first know that all that you experience fits with its intended journey for you, and it knows that you may not yet know how to become the source of self-validating acceptance and love for yourself. When you make what looks like mistakes, your soul knows, you will eventually get to the truth that you are cocreating all you experience and that you can bring acceptance and compassion to yourself in all phases of your life, including rewriting the meaning of the narrative attached to your apparent mistakes.

About the Author

Tom Jacobs is an evolutionary astrologer, energy worker, and channel. A Level II graduate of evolutionary astrologer Steven Forrest's Apprenticeship Program (member since 2004), he has a global practice of readings, coaching, and teaching people to understand what their souls sent them to Earth to do and supporting them in making it happen. Tom is the author of numerous books on astrology, mythology, and spirituality including six volumes of channeled material, and original astrological natal reports on Lilith, Chiron, and emotional healing. He also offers a variety of energetically programmed crystals and stones to stir and support opening, healing, balance, and release.

Contact Tom via http://tdjacobs.com or http://healingsuicide.com.

Printed in Great Britain
by Amazon